MW01240816

Product
Leadership

The Product Manager's Handbook

Jay Harel

Product Leadership

The Product Manager's Handbook

By Jay Harel

Cover and interior design by Jay Harel

Third Edition, published in 2022

ISBN-10 : 1494341263

ISBN-13 : 978-1494341268

Dedicated to the people who inspired me
and to those who will

Table of Contents

Introduction

I took on writing this book after looking for a practical guide for product managers and failing to find a well-written one that was useful, easily digestible, and relatively short. In order to stay true to my original intent of keeping it concise, I split this new and expanded edition into two separate books: Effective Product Management, a shorter book focusing on product management, and Product Leadership, which is longer and broader in scope.

This book covers the whole gamut of product management: it starts by discussing core skills such as effective communication, continues with basic tasks like backlog management, and covers more advanced topics like finding the right product to build. On top of that, it discusses the broader scope of work that product managers are involved in, including hiring, team management, sales, and marketing.

My book Effective Product Management is more concise and only covers the day-to-day aspects of the profession. It's a subset of this book, so you can skip it if you read this one.

By being lean on examples, this book embodies the imperative of focusing on what matters while ignoring the rest, which is often challenging to attain and maintain while managing products. I made every effort to keep the discourse as relevant and concise as possible. The book aims at helping product managers become more effective and productive while realizing that they are central nodes in today's networked organizations. In fact, product managers are so crucial, that without their concerted efforts, the work of engineers, marketers, salespeople, and others is often in vain.

What to Expect

This practical book will guide you along the roller-coaster ride of the product life cycle and walk you through the realities of being a product manager. You will find it useful whether you are a product manager or work with product management professionals. What you won't find here are didactic descriptions of various methodologies. Also absent are tedious instructions and standard operating procedures describing how to perform specific tasks; no one follows these anyway. Instead, the book consists of short, mostly independent chapters describing best practices and pointing out pitfalls to avoid. The sum total provides a clear sense of how to do product management right.

A Note on Terminology

I use the term Product Manager throughout the book, but it might as well be substituted with titles like Director of Product Management, VP of Product Management, VP of Product, Product Lead, Head of Product, Product Owner, Product Line Manager, Group Product Manager or Chief Product Officer. Brand Management is a close cousin; most of this book applies to it as well. Some companies use the term Program Manager to mean product manager. Others use it to refer to a project manager. This leads to confusion around what PM stands for, so I avoided using this acronym in this book. Product Marketing, also often shortened to PM, is sometimes used to describe what is essentially product management but more often refers to a branch of marketing. All of these titles fall under the "Product Management" umbrella covered here.

Most advice about managing products applies to product features, sets of features, and other parts of a larger product. It also applies to product lines or groups of products. A product line is merely a superset and has product features in and of itself. Furthermore, although I refer to products throughout the book, most of it applies to services as well. Services can (and should) be treated like products, complete with all the trimmings.

Who is this Book for?

This book draws on my two decades of experience in product management. While most insights come from business-to-business software product management, product managers in other disciplines will find it helpful as the methods and ideas outlined here are universal. Your experience level will determine what you gain by reading it:

- **Aspiring product managers**: this book shows you what product management is all about. It explores the good bits, highlights the challenges, and dispels misconceptions. Most of all, it describes the broad range of responsibilities that product management entails so you can make an informed decision before taking the plunge.

- **Novice product managers**: the book describes proven methods backed by years of experience and education. It will teach you shortcuts and show you how to avoid pitfalls as you grow your product management career.

- **Experienced product managers**: you already know much of the material covered in this book. However, I am confident you could use a refresher and learn some best practices in areas you may have paid less attention to over the years. These will make your product - and your life - better.

- **People who work with product managers**: engineers, marketers, executives, and others will learn about the intricacies of product management and how to achieve their goals more effectively when working with product managers.

Progress in product management is made in the trenches, with battle scars to show for it. This book touts a hands-on approach coupled with personal ownership, which I found to be the best way to grow in product management, regardless of your career stage.

About the Author

I am a product management leader living and working in Silicon Valley. For two decades, I have managed products and teams in various markets, including SaaS, security, enterprise software, networking, and consumer internet. An engineer by training, I spent the early part of my career coding and leading engineering teams. I managed many product life cycles and experienced the ups and downs of the journey. Like any good product manager, I am a constant learner and continuously evolve and improve my skills. I hope you will learn as much by reading this book as I did writing it.

Who Needs Product Managers

Product managers are the unsung heroes of the tech industry. They carry a significant load and seldom get credit for their work. You often hear about rockstar programmers, but rarely about superstar product managers. You meet salespeople in their spiffy suits and perfectly polished shoes, while product managers stay in the back in their jeans and t-shirt. I lost count of the times I've heard people insinuate that product management is less crucial than other functions. This opinion has been voiced for as long as the product management discipline has existed, and has been dispelled time and time again. People seem to think (hope?) that a software business could consist of engineers building products and salespeople selling them or customers buying them directly, with pretty much nothing in between. This fantasy of free information flow from customers to engineering to sales to customers looks great on paper but does not work in practice. Despite the challenges, product management is gaining popularity, and its ranks are getting filled by the best and the brightest.

It's easy to confuse product managers with middle managers, the latter being the butt of many jokes and the target of mass layoffs. Companies are trying to get rid of them in an effort to "cut the middleman" and "improve information flow." I salute this effort and agree that bureaucrats, time-wasters, and useless "managers" should be shown the door. Product managers, however, are the exact opposite. They are not empty suits or paper pushers, as portrayed in the 1999 film Office Space. They are the glue that holds everything together.

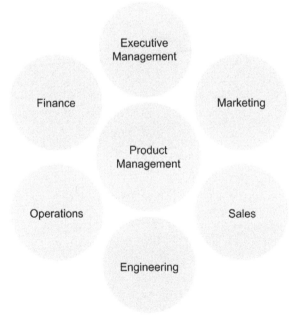

The central role of product management

The diagram above shows the central role that product management plays, serving as a hub and interacting with various other functions. Product managers are responsible for the *Why*, *What*, and *When*, while other stakeholders are responsible for the *How* and the *Who*. In this sense, product management is different from most other roles in a small tech company. More on this in the first part of the book.

Part 1

The Product Manager

The Product is your Business

As a product manager, the product is your business and you are its CEO. Chief Executive Officers can't afford to lose focus, ultimately being responsible for the success of their company and consequently for everything it takes to run it. CEOs live and breathe products, customers, sales, finance, strategy, competition, partnerships, technology, human resource management, and more. Realizing that product management is similar to general management makes it easier to visualize the magnitude of the task at hand.

Being a CEO involves a variety of challenges, including managing costs, opening new markets, motivating people, raising funds, and influencing decision-makers. CEOs masterfully juggle many balls, keeping all of them in the air. One of their biggest challenges, however, is staying focused. With a constant barrage of distractions, it's easy to concentrate on the tasks you feel more comfortable doing while taking your eye off the other balls.

CEOs don't have the luxury of dropping any ball. They must keep the business going at any cost (literally), either by delegating or by doing it themselves. Product management requires a similar degree of focus - focusing on the whole **and** its parts at the same time. It's not enough to be a "big picture thinker" or "detail-oriented"; you have to be both.

The overlap between CEOs and product managers

As the Venn diagram above shows, there's a significant overlap between the roles of CEOs and product managers. CEOs interact more with the outside world, while product managers are typically more technical and have a deeper understanding of the product. This diagram applies mainly to small technology companies; however, similar ones can be developed for other types of businesses. In general, the larger the company, the smaller the overlap.

The most important common element shared by CEOs and product managers is unwavering ownership and responsibility. CEOs are responsible for the overall success of the company, while product managers own the overall success of the product(s). In many cases, these goals are the same.

Thought Experiment

Chances are you go to conferences or trade shows, meet new people and exchange ideas. When you meet a new person, how long does it take for you to figure out what they do? Here's how it works for me:

- Salespeople: about three words.

- Engineers: about one sentence.

- Marketing people: about three sentences.

- Product managers: this one is tricky, and I often fail to get it right even after a few sentences. Being the multidisciplinary professionals that they are, product managers cover several domains and can speak multiple "languages."

What do Product Managers Actually do?

"People think focus means saying yes to the thing you've got to focus on. But that's not what it means at all. It means saying no to the hundred other good ideas."

- Steve Jobs

Product Managers are on a mission to build the right product. Achieving this is harder than it seems and involves countless tasks and steps. Pragmatic Marketing's annual survey[1] concludes that product managers are involved in an astounding number of activities. Here are their most frequent tasks in alphabetical order:

- Answering sales questions
- Articulating distinctive competencies
- Building customer acquisition plans
- Building customer retention plans

---

[1] https://www.pragmaticinstitute.com/resources/articles/product/annual-survey/

- Creating and updating the business plan
- Creating customer-facing sales collateral
- Creating internal sales tools
- Creating presentations and demos
- Defining buyer personas
- Defining the distribution strategy for the product
- Defining marketing plans
- Defining positioning
- Defining use scenarios
- Defining user personas
- Going on sales calls
- Launch planning
- Lead generation
- Maintaining the roadmap
- Making buy, build or partner decisions
- Managing innovation
- Managing product portfolios
- Market definition, sizing, and segmentation
- Measuring the ROI of marketing programs

- Monitoring product milestones
- Performing competitive analysis
- Performing technology assessment
- Performing win/loss analysis
- Providing sales channel training
- Setting and maintaining pricing
- Staffing seminar and trade show events
- Thought leadership
- Tracking product profitability (e.g., P&L)
- Understanding the customer's buying process
- Understanding market problems
- Writing product requirements
- Writing success stories

This is an impressively long list, but I can think of many other tasks, including participating in product architecture discussions, reviewing documentation, triaging bugs, and managing a team. One of the most critical responsibilities of a product manager is removing obstacles from their people's way in order to get stuff done. Great product managers do two things very well:

1. They move fast.

2. They are right most of the time.

The following chapters will explore many of these responsibilities in detail and describe the qualities that define effective product managers.

The Product Manager's Qualities

"Scientists solve problems that can be solved. Product Managers solve problems that have to be solved."

- Anonymous

The quote above captures the spirit of product management, the ultimate art of the possible. Effective product managers are not theoretical scientists. They must be 100% practical and focus on solving the problems at hand. Towards this end, they must possess several qualities. Here are the top five:

1. **Excellent communicator**
   Communicates effectively with everyone up and

down the organization and beyond. Delivers crisp and concise messages. Gets people. Intuitively understands human interaction, needs, aspirations, styles, and corporate politics. Interacts well with customers and partners. Can sell ideas and move people to action.

2. **Decisive**

Gets things done. Acts assertively and unequivocally. Makes tough decisions, often facing discord or ridicule. Doesn't hesitate much when choosing among several options and can quickly come up with new ideas as the situation evolves. Makes the right decision most of the time.

3. **Technical**

Understands the subject matter and can build rapport with the people who build the product. Effectively evaluates new technologies and ideas. Doesn't BS.

4. **Flexible**

Has a razor-sharp focus on the chosen course of action yet can quickly pivot and change direction when appropriate with no regrets or second thoughts. Can tolerate opposing views and deal effectively with conflicting facts.

5. **Operationally minded**

   Controls product life cycles from cradle to grave. Understands the machine-like qualities of a business and can contribute to all aspects of it, making it hum along more efficiently. Connects stakeholders and lubricates friction.

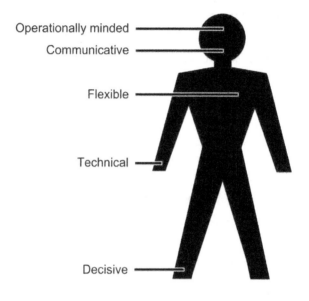

The product manager's top qualities

Bonus quality: **Dependable**. This last one allows you to move ahead in life and get promoted. It's expressed by delivering results instead of excuses. Steve Jobs said it well:

"Somewhere between the janitor and the CEO, reasons stop mattering... that Rubicon is crossed when you become a VP."

While a product manager needs to have all five essential qualities to be successful, having even one anti-quality will likely result in failure.

Anti-qualities:

1. **Lacks a backbone**
   Easily swayed and pushed around, unable to make decisions. Often hesitates and delays necessary actions until it's too late.

2. **Divisive**
   Demands instead of asking, derides instead of giving feedback, stabs others in the back instead of giving them a back massage. Pits people and teams against each other instead of being a catalyst for cooperation and progress.

3. **Clueless**
   Doesn't understand the subject matter, the market, the customer, the product, and the technology. Is slow on the uptake and cannot turn existing knowledge into new ideas.

4. **Inflexible**
   Paralyzed by perfectionism, unable to tell the

difference between the practical and the ideal. Overly conservative, lacking the free spirit essential for creating new concepts.

5. **Unorganized**

   Cannot keep track of multiple processes in parallel. Loses control of the situation when things get complicated. Can't see the forest for the trees.

Communication Skills

"I deal with the goddamn customers so the engineers don't have to. I have people skills! I am good at dealing with people. Can't you understand that? What the hell is wrong with you people?"

- Tom Smykowski, Office Space character

Communication skills are an essential requirement for every job nowadays, all the more so it comes to product management. In fact, it's arguably the most important skill for a product manager to have. Everything they do involves communication with other people. Every action they take results from good listening skills and has to be communicated to others. Their day revolves around communicating their ideas, requests, and plans to people up and down the chain, either individually or in group settings.

Modes of communication change through the years; how you do it and whomever the audience is, the goal is to **understand their real needs and desires** and **influence their actions**. There's no point in communicating without a clear goal because it wastes your time and theirs. Water cooler chats are fine, of course; don't be a hermit. However, continually saturating the ether with noise is not a good practice. Unfortunately, some people do this in a futile attempt to show how important they are. Much to their chagrin, no one gets rewarded for being a nuisance.

Focused and succinct communication is essential. Nobody wants to hear you ramble on end about this and that. Adapt your communication style to the setting and stakeholders involved. Case in point: your team members need you to be confident and reassuring but don't necessarily want a detailed analysis of loosely related topics. Your boss needs you to describe things as they are but doesn't want to know all the minute details (otherwise, why would they need you?).

Good communication skills are critical for product managers, as they regularly communicate with stakeholders across their company and beyond. Product managers are often called upon to deliver roadmap information to customers. Communicating with enterprise customers is exciting, but take the wrong turn, and you step into a minefield. Beyond the obvious – listen more than you speak, be engaging, and stay positive – it's important to observe experienced team members do it before taking the plunge.

What separates good communicators from bad ones? Characterizing bad communicators is easy: they act like pundits who dish out a blended brew of facts and opinions (or worse) while only pretending to be listening. Good communicators, on the other hand, have more subtle qualities.

Customers need you to understand their needs and offer trustworthy information about how your product or service can solve their problems. To do this well, you must start by listening intently. As you synthesize their input into your roadmap, you should give them clearly articulated information about what's coming down the pike and when, and what's being pushed out and why. There's room for marketing fluff, strategic hand-waving, opinionated punditry, and salesy over-promising, but it shouldn't come from product management. Customers expect you to be a knowledgeable and responsible adult with a deep understanding of the subject matter.

Honesty is better than sugar-coated bullshit. Customers want to hear the facts from a calm and composed product leader. Being able to do this well is positively correlated with effective product management in general. An effective product manager can leverage customer trust to collect actionable feedback that will make the product more sticky, up-sellable, supportable, adaptable, distinguishable, and technologically achievable.

Good communication skills extend beyond mere communication. They are a reflection of highly developed management and people skills. While speech impairments, accents, physical appearance, age, and other extraneous factors make it challenging for some people to identify good communicators, it's certainly worth the effort. A good communicator can always handle – indeed seek – feedback from anyone regardless of their position or title. Not only can they take it in, but they also are skilled in turning it into product and process improvements and, ultimately, business growth.

Key Communication Skills

1. **Listener**: Listens intently and understands the message, tone, and subtext. Reads the lines and what's in between. Avoids the trap of reading too much into things.

2. **Explainer**: Knows the audience and delivers a succinct message that fills the gaps in their knowledge and resonates with them.

3. **Pacifier**: Understands the dynamics of the situation and calmly speaks to the hearts of everyone involved, helping them to reach a productive resolution.

4. **Hostage negotiator**: Able to talk people out of precarious situations, getting them to climb down the ledge and rejoin the team.

5. **Connector**: Connects people with other people and ideas, creating a whole that is greater than the sum of its parts.

Listening

"When people talk, listen completely. Most people never listen."

- Ernest Hemingway

Listening to customers has never been more critical than in today's competitive environment. It can augment insights gleaned from usage data or stand on its own if other forms of data are unavailable, as in the case of a small, statistically insignificant sample. When listening to a customer, you often hear a story rather than a series of facts.

Stories are magical. Watching, hearing, or reading a good story can give you a distinct feeling that is difficult, expensive, or illegal to achieve otherwise. Good stories are easy to remember and relate to. Unfortunately, when gathering product feedback, the stories you hear are often dull, fragmented, vague, or repetitive. Just like listening to a bad story, customer feedback is easy to ignore and disregard. It can numb and lull you into preferring your preconceived notions over what the customer is telling you. Every so often, you come across an articulate customer who can distill the essence of their experience and report on it in a clear and concise way. Sometimes, however, you find yourself in front of a user who seems to insist on speaking off-topic and griping about a bevy of unrelated issues.

Salespeople know that success depends on being a good listener; product managers must be even better. It's crucial that you listen intently, not just hear what the other person is saying. You can only understand people you genuinely listen to. Try to dig out the message hidden between the lines, but don't be overly confident when separating signal from noise; the real gems may hide in plain sight.

Active listening is a tried and true technique for guaranteeing a high degree of comprehension. It's really more about forcing yourself to listen than getting the speaker to speak clearly. The idea is to repeat what the speaker says in your own words and then ask them if you faithfully represented their message. If they confirm, you move on. Otherwise, you try again or have them explain it in a different way. It can be slow and frustrating for both sides, but it works. A similar, more formal version is used in aviation. Pilots are required to read back flight controller instructions, and controllers, in turn, must listen to pilots reading back the instruction (often in abbreviated form) and verify that they repeated it correctly. If they did, the controller moves on. Otherwise, the controller repeats the instruction (often with an increasingly discernible tone of frustration) until the pilot reads it back correctly. This guarantees that both sides are on the same page and is designed to prevent a misunderstanding that can result in an accident.

Confirmation Bias, the tendency to agree with people who are like us and hold similar views, can skew our understanding and make us believe in things that aren't real while ignoring the facts. It's therefore vital to keep an open mind and fight the urge to resist opinions that go against our own. At the same time, it's crucial not to be tempted to accept opinions similar to ours blindly.

Filter bubbles exist not only on social media; try listening to as many customers as possible and giving your undivided attention not only to the squeaky wheels but to every relevant one. Listen intently and without bias, and you will gain priceless insights.

Writing

"If people cannot write well, they cannot think well, and if they cannot think well, others will do their thinking for them."

— *George Orwell*

Being able to express yourself clearly in writing is as crucial as ever. For decades, people lamented the decline in written communications. Then came the age of email, instant messaging, texting, and blogging. We now read and write more than ever; written business communication is essential and ubiquitous. It is so prevalent that it is safe to assume that it will not be replaced entirely any time soon by video, virtual reality, holograms, or any other futuristic technology. Email and messaging are used for anything and everything, including topics they were previously deemed inappropriate for, like salary discussions and business negotiations. Done right, these are great tools for any human communication, especially when preceded or followed by verbal (preferably in-person) interaction. It's important not to rely solely on email, chat, or text for critical communications. Avoid using these communication forms as a shield. They are ineffective for any kind of negativity, as they can be logged, forwarded, and haunt you forever.

Verbal communication is such an integral part of who we are that our brain reacts to it in a natural way. People have been reading and writing emails for so long that it's almost like their brains have been rewired to treat them like spoken language. Still, most people perceive it differently from verbal communication and may consequently receive a different message than intended. Write clearly and succinctly to prevent any unintended consequences. When emailing, focus on delivering facts; avoid trying to convey complex emotions. If you do, stick to positive ones like gratitude, humility, and happiness.

I suggest following a few guiding principles when "putting pen to paper." The best writing advice I have ever received is **no fluff**. Brevity trumps wordiness. Fluffiness wastes your time and, worse, your readers'. Mumbling is annoying and off-putting. Waxing poetic over this, that, and the other will not get you far.

Practical writing advice:

- After you are done writing, wait a while (at least a few hours, if possible), then edit and rewrite as required. Repeat as necessary.

- Practice. Then practice more. Then practice even more. Write anything on your mind on whatever you have handy - laptop, tablet, phone, or paper.

- Take a creative writing class. You are not likely to end up writing novels, but getting formal training in laying out your thoughts and ideas in writing wouldn't hurt.

- Write a new blog post every month/week/day - whatever works for you, as long as you write regularly and publish often.

- Refresh your grammar and punctuation skills and learn to avoid common mistakes. Use Grammarly (or similar), whether you are a native English speaker or not.

- Read a classic writing guide like The Elements of Style by William Strunk Jr.

Speaking

"Make sure your brain is in gear before engaging the mouth."

      -Bumper sticker wisdom

Speaking clearly and to the point is critically important, yet many fail to do it. Instead, they circle around and around, forcing their listeners to make an extra effort to understand the point. We all learn to speak at a very young age, but not all of us reach a mastery level. While the technical aspects of speaking are straightforward, translating thoughts into clear sentences is challenging for many people. They think clearly and have great ideas, but somewhere between their brains and their mouths, ideas lose their oomph and turn into mushy, mangled messages. It's a pity, as they don't get a fair chance to share their brilliance with others.

Here is some practical speaking advice:

- Speak up (but don't shout).

- Slow down (but don't crawl).

- Join Toastmasters or find other ways to practice speaking in front of an audience and get immediate, honest feedback.

- If you're lucky enough to get honest feedback, apply it, and get better at converting thought trains into word sequences and sentence progressions.

- Not a native English speaker? Ask trusted friends to comment on your diction and help improve your enunciation and pronunciation, focusing on the syllables that your accent impacts the most.

- Delivering a clear message over the phone can be challenging. Without visual cues, it isn't easy to gauge feedback; you can't wave your hands to make a point. Be aware of the shortcomings and overcome them by asking listeners to confirm their understanding.

Presenting

"No audience ever complained about a presentation or speech being too short."

— *Stephen Keague*

Business presentations are a tool for driving people to take action. They aren't meant to entertain, unless this is part of your tactic. For a product manager, delivering a message is not interesting in and of itself. The only reason to take other people's time and have them listen to you (in a conference room or across the internet) is to move them to take a desirable action like buying, building, marketing, partnering, selling, or funding your product. There are two ways to present effectively and a less effective one that is, unfortunately, more common.

Storytelling: The human brain reacts to good stories. Stories activate our emotions, and this helps to cement the message in our minds. Whenever possible, tell a story. Remember the first rule of writing, though: no fluff. Telling a story doesn't give you a license to waste your audience's time. If your message can be storified, great; otherwise, don't force it.

Visuals: *A picture is worth a thousand words* is a good rule of thumb. Photos, diagrams, and illustrations are a great way to deliver a succinct message - if you have the right ones. Finding images online and sprinkling them throughout your presentation is not a magic solution. Telling a good story in pictures requires more effort than writing it. Animation can help tell a story but use it sparingly because it can quickly feel excessive. Video is a great medium; however, producing a good one is prohibitively expensive (in terms of time and money) for most product management needs.

Bullet points: Most people overuse bullet points, cramming heaps of them into overcrowded slides. They commit this sin mainly because it's so easy to do it mindlessly. Just because everybody does it, it doesn't mean that it's right for you. Guy Kawasaki's 10/20/30 rule is a helpful mnemonic for avoiding this trap: No more than ten slides, taking no longer than twenty minutes, using a thirty-point font. No need to take this literally, but using fewer slides and large fonts will force you to be more succinct and ensure that the text is readable.

When crafting your slide deck, focus on storytelling, and use relevant visuals. The fewer bullet points you use, the more memorable your pitch will be.

Negotiating

*"When arguing with a fool,
make sure they are not doing
the same"*

- Anonymous

For product managers, the ratio of responsibility to authority is off the chart. More often than not, the only tool at their disposal is their ability to talk people into taking action - people over whom they have no authority whatsoever.

This is where good negotiators shine. Being able to articulate your needs and wants and working your way to a win-win outcome takes a considerable amount of practice.

Here are some negotiation tips:

- Listen more than you talk.

- Never ignore or dismiss the other side's position.

- Read between the lines, but don't read too much into it.

- Be aware of the other side's alternatives, and make sure you fully understand yours.

- You can always benefit from being a pacifier and helping dueling parties reach an agreement.

Being an experienced negotiator and sporting battle scars can help you avoid negotiating in the first place. A clear roadmap can help you achieve that.

When it comes to feature requests, product managers are in what may seem to the untrained eye as an absolute power position. They are often the ones who say no and force others to come up with convincing reasons for implementing certain features. Requests come from all around the organization, primarily from customer-facing folks in sales, professional services, customer support, sales engineering, marketing, and the like.

It's easy to answer every request with a "no" or a "later," but you can't keep doing this forever. Sooner or later, you will have to face reality and make tough decisions. Until this stage arrives, don't just say no; provide plausible reasoning and verify that the person on the receiving end understands your point. If you are flooded with requests, create a long-term roadmap and a short-term feature list (a backlog) that all stakeholders can view. It won't keep the fire away forever, but the improved visibility can do wonders. It will enable you to sidestep arguments as others will perceive the published roadmap as a stake in the ground and make them think twice before contesting it. After all, winning the battle before it even starts is the essence of the art of war.

Read more about publishing a roadmap in the chapter Publishing a Roadmap and about grooming it in the Backlog Management chapter.

Managing Details

"If you don't understand the details of your business, you are going to fail."

- Jeff Bezos

One of the product manager's essential superpowers is increasing clarity by summarizing countless details and turning them into succinct information nuggets. Being able to package these ideas for different audiences, such as engineering, sales, and executive management, is the icing on the cake. In fact, attention to detail is so crucial that no one should be allowed into product management unless they excel in it. You need to see the forest **and** the trees, making sense of thousands of minute items by fitting them into a larger picture. But even the best sometimes feel dwarfed by the never-ending tsunami of (often conflicting) details.

The only cure is to anticipate the flood and prepare for it. By doing so, you will demonstrate that you have what it takes to manage your time and your product. Plan ahead and act: get more resources, delegate if it makes sense, and say "no" more often. Whatever you do, you must plan in advance. Ad-hoc measures are more likely to fail. You can also choose to overwork yourself to death, but it's not sustainable and doesn't reflect well on your management legacy.

The adage "you can't manage what you can't measure" applies to detail management. To get your house in order, develop a methodology for organizing the details that come your way. Bugs, feature backlogs, customer feedback, strategic plans, and abstract ideas should be captured and organized neatly, preferably in a system that allows for easy sharing. Having it well organized will allow you to measure and manage progress. You will be able to quickly answer questions like "how many new feature requests did we get last month," and "how often do we pivot our strategic direction."

Decision-making is an acquired skill, and the best decision-makers can not only make quick decisions, but make the right ones quickly. As a product manager, you are judged by how fast you can make up your mind and how accurate your decisions are. Neither is sufficient by itself; taken together, they provide a pretty good heuristic of your effectiveness.

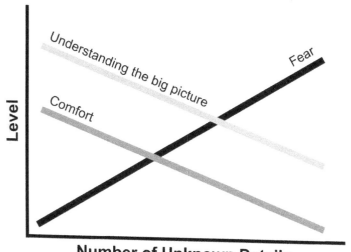

The less you know, the more afraid you are

To state the obvious, one aspect that is difficult to measure and manage is the unknown. While being flooded with details can be overwhelming, realizing that there are many that you are not even aware of is scary. As the simplified diagram above shows, fear increases as the mystery grows. Being afraid of the unknown is only natural. Like many things in life, it is challenging and exciting at the same time.

Embrace it and be at peace with it, and you will become more creative and innovative. Fear itself will not kill you; it's where the best ideas often come from (for more on dealing with fear, read the chapter *Embrace the Fear*).

An increasing lack of knowledge hurts your big-picture view. At some point, you must stop and decide whether it's too risky to continue. It happens when the strategy becomes so fuzzy that carrying on doesn't make sense anymore. Where exactly to draw this line depends on many factors and is one of the most difficult decisions a product manager has to make. To this end, business savvy, technical aptitude, and intuition can be of great help. More on these in the next chapters.

Business Savvy

"When the wind blows, some people build walls, others build windmills."

- Chinese proverb

To be successful, product managers should have a deep understanding of the market they play in. The better you understand it, the more effective your product decisions will be. Understanding the market requires having a clear big-picture view and a good grasp of business dynamics.

Some people are lucky enough to watch their parents run businesses or grow up in an environment encouraging entrepreneurship. Others try and fail several times, learning by doing. Many go to business school hoping to acquire these skills, and some learn by watching their friends or colleagues do it or by reading business books voraciously. Whichever way you go about learning it, the goal is the same: developing an intuitive understanding of how business works in your market, how goods and services are bought and sold, how companies run efficiently, and how they cope with dynamic market forces.

At the end of the day, your experience is your best guide to becoming a good business person. Remember that everything has a price and is negotiable. One commodity that should raise a red flag is the integrity of people who are unscrupulous enough to compromise it. Stay away from them if at all possible. If you have no choice but to deal with them, seek help from battle-scarred colleagues or mentors.

A common thread across all thriving businesses is a whirlwind of action: fierce competition, urgent customer demands, impossible deadlines, and strong-minded people, to name a few. Business savvy requires a level of maturity that enables you to deal with adversity and manage crises effectively. Whatever happens, remain in control. Be calm and composed no matter what. **You are a leader of people**, even if you don't have direct authority over them. **You are a business person**, even if you're not in sales. **You are your product's CEO**, even if you feel small and powerless. Ignore the noise and push forward. If it doesn't kill you, it makes you stronger.

Technical Aptitude

"Technical skill is mastery of complexity, while creativity is mastery of simplicity."
    - Erik Christopher Zeeman

While product managers don't need a technical background, it certainly helps. Technical aptitude will help you converse in the language of the people building the product without sounding or feeling clueless. It will make your life easier, especially if you work closely with engineers or researchers. Technical professionals have rich jargon and are sometimes impatient with people who don't understand them right away. Speaking their language will make you more accessible, and that's a good thing.

If you don't have a technical background, don't despair. Whether your company makes contact lenses, cloud software, advertising platforms, or aerospace components, it's not rocket science (except for the latter, maybe). You're not going to be designing and building the actual products; what you need to know is learnable. You must work hard and learn quickly without overlooking your other duties.

Being "technical" is often not enough; some companies expect candidates to have a technical background in a specific field. This approach often stems from laziness, inertia, or a desire to put less effort into training, hoping the new person will hit the ground running. In reality, this rarely predicts a new product manager's effectiveness. Domain expertise can have a negative effect, too. For example, a candidate who worked at a poorly managed company in your space may bring these poor management practices along.

Technical abilities are transferable from one field to another. Good technical people know what they know because they learned how to learn. They can absorb new concepts quickly and apply them successfully in their practice. This bodes well with product management since product managers are constant learners. Indeed, product management is - in many ways - a technical occupation. With or without a technical background, however, you can be successful at it if you work hard enough.

Intuition

"My biggest regrets are the moments that I let a lack of data override my intuition on what's best for our customers."
- Andrew Mason
after leaving the CEO
position at Groupon

On a job interview a while back, I uttered the one word you don't want to mention on that occasion - especially when the interviewer is an ex-Googler: "intuition." Interviewers want to hear about your analytical and well-reasoned thinking skills, not about nebulous concepts like intuition. That interview was the last in a series of eight and was supposed to seal the deal.

The question I was answering was about my approach to product management and, more specifically, how I make decisions on challenging issues with conflicting requirements. I rambled on about "looking carefully at the data," "analyzing customer input," "evaluating feature profitability," and other serious-sounding sound bites, and then said that after thoroughly evaluating all the inputs, I sometimes have to make a decision based on my intuition. The interviewer paused and repeated, "intuition?" At that moment, I knew that I had lost that job opportunity.

Was mentioning "intuition" a mistake? Yes. Does intuition have a place in the workplace? Absolutely, if you accept the following definition attributed to Abella Arthur: "Intuition is a combination of historical (empirical) data, deep and heightened observation and an ability to cut through the thickness of surface reality. Intuition is like a slow-motion machine that captures data instantaneously and hits you like a ton of bricks. Intuition is a knowing, a sensing that is beyond the conscious understanding - a gut feeling. Intuition is not pseudo-science."

Every decision we make is based, at least in part, on our intuition or "gut feeling." People who cannot intuit tend to get stuck when faced with reams of data. Analysis Paralysis is one of the worst enemies of effective execution. I'm not talking about the obvious cases, where data analysis can lead to an eventual clear decision, but about situations where:

1. A decision must be made

    and,

2. The data does not point in any particular direction and may, in fact, lead to conflicting conclusions.

People who can use their intuition effectively shine in these situations. Intuition allows them to improvise successfully when they have no other choice. It's particularly crucial in a startup environment; if you can't act on your gut feeling, you can quickly analyze yourself out of existence. Let's face it; sometimes, the only course of action is to wing it. For example, you may be asked tough questions at a customer meeting. If you don't know the answers, protocol dictates that you promise to get back to them. If they keep prodding, however, you may eventually be compelled to provide some answers. A healthy intuition will enable you to provide answers that are surprisingly close to what you would have provided had you had the opportunity to analyze the situation or consult an expert.

We all intuit every day, but it's imperative to be very careful about it. That "gut feeling" can easily lead you astray. Daniel Kahneman, the economics Nobel Prize laureate, talks in his book Thinking, Fast and Slow about the growing body of research demonstrating our two modes of thinking or two "systems." One intuitive and quick, the other rational and slow. We have adapted to drawing quick conclusions based on our experience when faced with tough choices. Those decisions are mostly right, but not always. The problem is that we often don't know we are wrong. That's when the "slow" path comes in handy, allowing us to analyze the data at hand and deduce educated conclusions, thus increasing the likelihood of finding the correct answer. An effective product manager knows when to think "fast" or "slow" and when is the right moment to switch between the two.

Flow

We all know the feeling of getting absorbed in our work and forgetting the world around us. Psychologists call it *flow*. Some call it *being in the zone*. It's that magical feeling you get when you are fully immersed in an activity with seemingly endless energy, totally consumed by and focused on the task at hand. A sense of complete absorption that feels almost like a transcendental experience. A state of consciousness that is so smooth that things seem to be running on autopilot.

How do you get there? Not by taking controlled substances or overdosing on caffeine. As a product manager, you get there after acquiring a certain amount of experience in managing your product. You get there by being very good at what you do. There are no prescriptions or shortcuts. If you haven't experienced it yet, keep at it; eventually, it will just happen, and you will find yourself in the most blissful flow.

Like intuition, flow can backfire. Programmers experience it when chasing a stubborn bug, losing themselves in a world of code and data, and going deeper and deeper down the rabbit hole. Before they know it, several hours have gone by. The downside of this intense concentration is that they may get myopic and waste precious time going down the wrong path.

Product managers, many of whom come from engineering roles in a past life, are accustomed to this MO. What's a product manager to do? Go with the flow but pull yourself out now and then and look around you. Take a walk, drink water, talk to people, read an interesting article, or just breathe some fresh air. It will break the flow all right, but the energy boost will help you think out of the box and make tangible progress when you dive back in.

Attitude

"Whether you think you can or you think you can't - you're right."

- Henry Ford

Product managers have as many dreams as responsibilities. They wish they could decide what their product would be like without the burden of customer requests, management dicta, and engineering pushbacks. They wish they could decide what's best for the customer and get it implemented with no qualms. They wish they could just do it.

While these are healthy desires, they conflict with virtually all acceptable product management processes. These processes tend to follow the curve rather than create it. Reactive product management goes with the flow, innovating here and there. On the other hand, proactive product management often goes against the axiom "The customer is always right" and sets the tone rather than following an unseen conductor.

Theoretically-perfect product managers have two convictions:

1. I know what product to build.

2. I will make it happen.

These are noble goals to aspire to, but they are rarely achieved consistently by mere mortals. Steve Jobs, Elon Musk, and a few others come to mind as people who managed to do it over long periods of time, but even they had their ups and downs.

Effective product managers know that while often right, the customer doesn't always know what they need. They can read between the lines of human interaction and analytics reports. They understand the market and can figure out what the winning product should be. They create action plans and execute them without getting discouraged by implementation woes. They push their vision forward and get customers to want the product. They are always right.

The rest of us employ a mix of fact-based decision making and intuitive reasoning. Virtually all product management literature touts the need to "listen to the pulse of the market," "nurture customer feedback," and "trust the data." Until you reach the level of the demigods mentioned above, you are bound to follow this advice.

Coping with the realization that we're not perfect can be challenging and frustrating. Keeping at it consistently over a long time requires the right attitude - an attitude that comes from within and projects outward. A Zen-like approach will allow you to deal with the emotional strain and ultimately be right more often than not. Combined with consistency and dedication, it will get you closer to becoming an ideal product manager. More on persistence in the next chapter.

The Nuts and Bolts of Persistence

"Success requires a persistent misreading of the odds."

- Tom Peters

Effective product managers are persistent but not obsessive. Obsessive people are often caustic and annoying, qualities that can quickly become roadblocks when trying to influence others. Persistence, however, is crucial for successful product management. Here's a little story about how I learned valuable lessons about persistence and perseverance from sorting thousands of small items.

After who-knows-how-many years of collecting bolts, nuts, washers, nails, and other metal knick-knacks (don't ask me why), I finally decided to sort them all into neat little drawers. The task was formidable; I must have had more than 10,000 of them. Picking and placing each one in the right drawer looked like it would take forever. I started regardless, and a strategy revealed itself as I progressed. The lessons I learned apply to many other seemingly impossible goals:

1. Start doing whatever you need to do; sooner or later, you will figure out how to do it better. Experience is your best teacher.

2. Take a utilitarian approach. Determine which items are the most useful and start with them, as they are more likely to yield the biggest bang for the buck.

3. It's not going to be perfect. Accept this fact and don't obsess over it.

4. Optimize the number of categories you will use - the smaller it is, the faster the sorting process will be. In the long run, however, it will be harder to find specific items if you only have three drawers labeled "Bolts," "Nuts," and "Misc."

5. Sorting can take a while, and your attention will tend to drift as you go along. Be clear and consistent about what goes into each drawer, or you will end up with a bigger mess and more wasted time.

6. Dump the rusty nails and crooked screws. There's no point wasting your energy on them unless it takes less than two seconds to wipe off some dirt masquerading as rust. If a nail is rusty, it's not going

to get un-rusty. If it's bent, you will spend a while banging on it, trying to straighten it up, only to find out that it's still not perfectly straight. If the threads on a screw are not even, you will regret keeping it when you find a use for it. The bottom line: with so many items at hand, you can always find a better one. Just dump the rejects.

7. Having said that, the fewer items of a specific kind, the more valuable each one is. If the number of items is small enough to make each one count, see if you can fix, groom, and develop them. If an item is hopelessly screwed up, you'd be better off dumping it and getting another one instead.

8. You don't have the resources to build the ultimate sorting machine, but wouldn't it be fantastic? Imagine this giant contraption: you place a random nut in the hopper, and it fetches a matching bolt in two seconds flat. Maybe you will build it one day, but for now - back to work.

9. Some items won't fit in any category, but creating a new one for each one-of item doesn't make sense. Table them for now and revisit this decision later.

10. It takes less time than you think. Start working and hone your skills as you go. You will be over and done with it before you know it.

With all the creativity and agility that product managers apply to their job, doing some monotonous or mindless work has meditative qualities that provide a good balance. Review somebody else's document, revise a financial model for the 12th time, or give yet another demo of the same product feature. These tasks may be tedious and repetitive but can free your mind to do more meaningful work.

Product Focus

"If you keep your eye on the profit, you're going to skimp on the product. But if you focus on making really great products, then the profits will follow."

- Steve Jobs

Shareholders want you to focus on the bottom line, looking to maximize their investment. Long-term investors are more tolerant of focusing on growth for a while, but if the company doesn't generate a profit, they, too, will eventually get antsy. However desirable it may be, focusing on the bottom line can backfire and get customers, employees, and others at odds with you. Worse, it may lead you to do whatever it takes to increase profit: compromising on quality, cutting shady distribution deals, using questionable marketing techniques, or worse.

With only the bottom line in your gun sight, you are bound to ship inferior products. Instead, focus on the product itself. Your customers will be more satisfied, employees will love to work for your company, and eventually, the bottom line will smile back at you.

One of your goals as a product manager is to ensure that your company understands how important it is to put the product front and center. It's good for the company and great for you. Product-focused companies are heaven for product managers. If you are in such a company, you know what I'm talking about. If you're not that lucky, make it your goal to reorient the company and get decision-makers to realize the benefits.

Tastemaking

"Knowing what you can not do is more important than knowing what you can do. In fact, that's good taste."

- A. C. Benson

Product management is an obscure art. Many people, especially outside the tech world, have no clue what it really is. When I tell an "outsider" what I do, they often reply, "You mean project management?" The lengthy explanation that follows sometimes falls on deaf ears.

For a more compelling explanation, it is helpful to use a short statement that anyone can relate to, like "a product manager is an x for y." The object (y) represents the product's overall experience or quality. Even if the product doesn't have any visible user interface (like an API or an internal power supply), it is a part of something people use, and their experience is the ultimate goal. But what is the subject (x)? Before we get into that, let's talk about taste.

taste

a: critical judgment, discernment, or appreciation

b: manner or aesthetic quality indicative of
such discernment or appreciation

After all the data is processed, customers consulted, competitors studied, and engineers brainstormed, the essence of product management is to use good judgment and make the right roadmap decision. In other words - and referencing the dictionary definition - a product manager should have good taste. Not just general taste; a good taste in the subject matter and the market they play in. Good product managers are connoisseurs in their field.

con·nois·seur

an expert judge in matters of taste.

Outstanding product managers are tastemakers, setting a trajectory and influencing others to develop good taste as well. This brings us to the ultimate definition: an effective product manager is a tastemaker for user experience.

taste·mak·er

a person who decides or influences what is or
will become fashionable.

Crosscheck: Steve jobs is considered one of the best product managers ever. "User experience tastemaker" is an apt way to summarize his achievements. Paul Graham, a great thinker and co-founder of Y Combinator, published an excellent post on the topic several years ago[2].

Product Mismanagement

"Making mistakes is human. Repeating 'em is too."

- Malcolm Forbes

If there were an Ig Nobel prize for product management, it should be awarded to product managers who march blindly toward failure. Those who toil endless hours (and have others do the same) to build a product that no one needs or one that doesn't do what it's supposed to do. After all, this great resource spend should be honored in some way, and the market will certainly not give them any accolades.

Every time I see a dead-on-arrival product, I think to myself, "someone must have known about this well in advance" - especially if it's not one of the first few iterations. That

---

[2] http://www.paulgraham.com/taste.html

someone should be the product manager, and if they didn't see it coming, they are twice at fault.

During the Obama administration, the government created a new website for streamlining sign-ups for the Affordable Care Act. The ensuing healthcare.gov debacle became a public example of a DOA product launch; other failures remain in the dark. As large a project as that one was, someone - a product manager or whatever their title was - must have been tasked with seeing the big picture and understanding the details. Or maybe there wasn't such a person (or people) assigned? Scary thought.

Product management usually gets little visibility, positive or negative, other than among those closely involved in creating the product. It's a shame because product managers contribute to significant achievements and spectacular failures. These often make for great stories, seldom told outside of the company. Such a waste of notoriety; someone ought to write a book about it.

The next part of the book deals with finding a product worth focusing on. Among other topics, we will discuss feedback analysis, design considerations, prioritization, and curation.

Part 2
The Right Product

Product Management Ain't Easy

Product management is difficult to define succinctly. My favorite definition is: "The role of the product manager is to discover the right product to build and facilitate its creation and commercialization." This part of the book will focus on the first part: discovering the right product to build.

Product managers advocate for users and make things happen on their behalf. Toward this end, they must first understand the product's raison d'être. The multi-stage discovery process includes the following:

- Developing a plan.
- Searching for clues.
- Gathering data.
- Leveraging multiple resources.
- Experimenting with different options.
- Collecting feedback.

- Following the right (and wrong) tracks.

- Putting the puzzle pieces together.

- Summarizing the results.

- Repeating the entire process as necessary.

Add working with (sometimes difficult) people and leading with no formal authority, and you get a good picture of the challenges involved.

We'll start the journey by describing the elements of the discovery process, starting with data gathering.

Customer Feedback

"If I had asked people what they wanted, they would have said faster horses."

—Henry Ford

"Listen to the voice of the customer." "The customer is always right." "Customer first." These popular truisms are true indeed, but they miss one crucial fact: the customer doesn't always know what they need. They certainly have an opinion and are sometimes very adamant about it, but it's up to you to decide what the product is and what features it will have. Deciding on a new feature just because a customer says they want it is an excuse used by inexperienced product managers, often resulting in a product that looks like a patchwork rather than an artwork.

Look beyond customer feedback to create a winning product

Don't get me wrong: the customer is always right, but it's your duty as a product manager to weigh your opinion against all other inputs and consider resource availability and allocation before making a decision that will influence the product. Only you can decide whether to accept their suggestions when piecing together the product puzzle. Only you can see all the details clearly enough to determine to what degree "the voice of the customer" fits in the grand scheme of things.

Your vision and the current state of affairs in your target market are no less important than customer feedback. Your decisions may be very difficult (or even impossible) for customers to stomach, and you may be called upon to explain and clarify your reasoning; this is part of the deal. Regardless, shaping the future of your product is ultimately your call, not the customer's.

The Customer is Always Right, Right?

A point of view can be a dangerous luxury when substituted for insight and understanding.
                    - Marshall McLuhan

The customer is always right, period.

If you have one customer, your life as a product manager is relatively easy – just do what they ask you to do. If you have millions of customers, use statistical analysis to figure out what product to build. The middle range is where it gets more challenging. Product managers acting in the lower range of that spectrum (typically in B2B companies) must be able to synthesize conflicting data into coherent roadmap decisions. A lot of this data comes directly or indirectly from customers, but usage data is often too limited to drive generalized conclusions. Product managers must have excellent listening skills, high emotional intelligence, and an ability to read between the lines.

In their frame of reference, the customer is always right

Customers know their business best and can articulate their needs better than anybody else. They pay your salary, so you effectively work for them. In reality, you can't do exactly what they want you to, even if your company's website states that you are "customer-driven" and are "committed to meeting your customers' expectations." Don't mistake marketing fluff for a roadmap strategy.

> Consider a humble chair. Now, put yourself in the shoes of a product manager tasked with creating a better one. Talking to customers, you find out that they want their chairs to have softer cushions, adjustable height, and lighter weight. Oh, and one customer would like it decorated with polka dots.

In your frame of reference, the customer is mostly right

A product leader must take into account the broader picture and consider a vast array of factors. Customer opinions matter more than others', but their input must inevitably be weighed against everything else that goes into the decision-making process. In many cases, it won't agree with your eventual decision. The real challenge is to find a way to accept their ideas without derailing strategic efforts. While making the right decision is often challenging, communicating it may be even harder. Treading a fine line between disappointing and satisfying customers requires experience and sound business senses.

Back to our chair: you have almost as many different requests as customers, but your company makes only one type of chair. Clearly, one chair doesn't fit all. What's a product manager to do? While your task is to improve on that chair, after analyzing the feedback, you realize that you can only satisfy a few customers at best. Ironically, the least reasonable request is the easiest to implement – a simple change to the painting process.

The customer being right doesn't solve your biggest problem

Innovation comes from engineers, researchers, designers, and others whose job is to create new things. They collaborate well and produce meaningful results when they get the information they need and have effective processes to follow. Your job is to articulate the goal and work with the team to prioritize the work based on customer feedback and feasibility considerations. Orchestrating innovation is your job number one, not the customers'.

> As a Chair Product Manager, you don't have to figure it all out by yourself. You certainly shouldn't make a decision based on partial, conflicting data. First, gather information about the competition and the partner ecosystem, study feasible manufacturing processes and potential materials, and collect all the data you can put your hands on. Next, articulate the goal and set creativity in motion, leveraging the effective processes you helped put in place. The collective ingenuity of the various stakeholders is the key to figuring this one out.

Product management is the art of the possible. It bridges the gap between customer needs and implementation constraints. It takes courage, experience, and creativity to do it well. Product managers must trust their instincts and the data they painstakingly collect and analyze. They are measured by their ability to find the right balance between contradicting demands, not by their ability to please everyone. In a perfect world, data is always trustworthy, and product managers always make the right decision. In our world, however, while the customer is always right, product managers aren't.

> Being the effective product manager that you are, you successfully harnessed the wisdom of your extended team and brought this furniture fable to a happy ending. While the team couldn't improve on all aspects of the product at the same time, you managed to take it up a notch. There's always one more version!

Regardless of the solution, you must be able to justify your decision

Product managers fill the gap between the customer's frame of reference and theirs with clear messaging, articulating the reasons for any discrepancy. They describe the plans to close the gap and support the reasoning behind their decision with data. Whether the customer is right or not, product managers must grow the business while fostering collaboration and communicating effectively with everyone. This often includes going back to a customer and letting them know that you are unable to deliver on their request. Doing this well while helping grow sales and reduce costs separates top product management performers from the rest.

Discovering the Right Product

"The greatest obstacle to discovery is not ignorance - it's the illusion of knowledge."
- Daniel J. Boorstin

Effective product managers are perceptive listeners and constant learners who know that the key to discovering the right product is asking the right questions. These come in different flavors:

- Asking existing and potential customers.

- "Asking" the data.

- Asking yourself.

To get actionable answers, you must ask specific questions. Nebulous questions result in fuzzy responses. When people reply to a general question with a specific answer, it should raise a warning flag. Specific answers usually focus on a narrow example and should be treated as merely a data point. Any answer is arguably biased, but specific responses to general questions are more likely to be so. Your job is to weed out the colorful opinions and focus on the noteworthy answers.

The following graph shows how the relative value of questions increases with specificity. Unfortunately, the number of people who can answer these questions decreases accordingly because fewer and fewer people know and understand the specifics. Needless to say, asking the wrong person will do you no good.

Likelihood of getting actionable answers
Number of people who can answer

Question types and their relative value

Running experiments is usually better than asking questions. Well-designed experiments allow you to control for biases and get better results. A/B tests and other studies based on actual usage are the best. Test results and auxiliary data must be examined and analyzed carefully; more on that in later chapters. Market research and focus groups are less effective as they are more likely to suffer from the "bad question syndrome" described earlier. The better the question, the better the answer.

As much as asking others and analyzing data is difficult, asking yourself is the most challenging. You have inherent biases resulting from years of experience and thousands of past decisions. You probably experienced similar situations months or years earlier and opted for a particular course of action. Your brain is now looking for similarities and trying to steer you toward a decision that worked for you in the past. However, the current situation is probably different. The more mistakes you've made in the past, the less likely you are to make one now. Still, questioning your own opinion and forcing yourself to go against your experience is very hard. This level of agility and introspection is a hallmark of highly effective product managers.

Data

"You can't always get what you want, but if you try sometimes, you just might find you get what you need."
- *The Rolling Stones, You Can't Always Get What You Want*

For product managers, data is like water. It sustains them and allows them to thrive. They need a constant supply of fresh data in order to shine, and just like murky water, bad data can ruin their day or even kill their product. With their data supply dwindling, a product manager may be forced to go forage for more, or worse, divine insights like a psychic instead of drawing educated conclusions.

Good product managers don't have to speculate whether it's good to rely on credible data when making decisions. No one in their right mind asks, "Shall I avoid liquids today and get parched?" Effective product managers seek and find data to corroborate their decisions and don't let any decision go unsupported unless they have no choice.

If you don't have enough data to decide which features to build, add data collection and analysis to the product itself. Holding off on releasing the product until you come across some useful information is not the solution; it will result in even less data being available to you. If you have no other choice, consider delaying the release until data collection is built into the product.

If the product is not stable enough, build better testing into the process and consider including the customer in it. Not letting the product out the door might extend its adolescence period because you are less likely to fix the most critical problems.

In reality, having high-quality data to base your decisions on is a luxury. Very often, collecting quality data is too expensive or otherwise impractical. And if you do have it, you have to analyze and turn it into actionable - hopefully enlightening - information. The less structured the data you collect is, the more challenging it is to analyze it. Make sure you don't spend considerable amounts of money collecting mountains of data that will only have a marginal effect on your product's market performance.

When looking at the results of your data analysis, be careful not to fall into the false accuracy trap and clearly understand causality. We'll discuss these issues and how to deal with them in the following chapters.

If all else fails, having a good story can replace hard data when talking someone into doing something. Solid, actionable data is worth its weight in gold, but gold is never cheap.

Correlation does not Imply Causation

"Reality is that which, when you stop believing in it, doesn't go away."

- Philip K. Dick

Blindly believing in what you want to happen can be dangerous. Your potential customers liked your demo? They may not like the actual product. Even if they do, they may not be willing to pay for it. Even if they promise they will buy it, you can't be sure they will - until the money is in the bank. In general, you can't conclude that one event causes another just because it happened in relative proximity, or because it "looks like" it's going to happen, or because you wish it will, or because it inflates your ego. In other words: correlation does not imply causation.

Correlation is dangerous. It can lull you into believing in things that aren't real. It may fool you into building a house of cards based on false - yet believable - assumptions. Resist the urge to jump to conclusions: check every assumption and corroborate every leap of faith from one fact to the next. If you can't prove it, don't use it.

Dr. Harriet Hall coined the term Tooth Fairy Science[3], referring to research based on unfounded "facts." She writes: "You could measure how much money the Tooth Fairy leaves under the pillow, whether she leaves more cash for the first or last tooth, whether the payoff is greater if you leave the tooth in a plastic baggie versus wrapped in Kleenex. You can get all kinds of good data that is reproducible and statistically significant. Yes, you have learned something. But you haven't learned what you think you've learned because you haven't bothered to establish whether the Tooth Fairy really exists."

When mining data to uncover actionable information, make sure you know what you are doing or ask someone who does. I'm sure you took statistics in college, but this was years ago. You can fall into the Tooth Fairy Science trap even if you're a math wizard or a statistical science black belt.

There's no magic formula for avoiding this trap; you must be careful. Take the time to get to the bottom of things and

---

[3] http://skepdic.com/toothfairyscience.html

understand the entire sequence of reasoning that leads from raw data to conclusions. Only then can you be sure that your actions are based on facts, not fiction.

Accuracy does not Imply Usefulness

*"Knowledge is a deadly friend
when no one sets the rules."*
- King Crimson,
Epitaph

We rely on predictive models because they are valuable tools for managing the future. And much like other tools, models can backfire. As George P. Box quipped, "All models are wrong, but some are useful."

When you pay a consultant a hefty sum to develop a detailed analysis of some key business area, the results may be impressively accurate but utterly useless. Consider the graph below, for example. It shows IDC's Intel Itanium chip sales forecasts made in nine consecutive years and the actual sales numbers; the difference is staggering. The sad part is that smart people paid good money to get these wrong forecasts, and they did so repeatedly, expecting different (better?) results. That's the definition of insanity, according to Albert Einstein.

Intel Itanium sales forecasts and the year they were published. Actual numbers are all the way at the bottom.

But what about "real" facts? What about "looking at the data" – querying, analyzing, summarizing, and all that good stuff? No matter how much effort you put into getting quality data, accuracy can easily be mistaken for usefulness. Paul Graham tells this story: "I remember telling David Filo in late 1998 or early 1999 that Yahoo should buy Google because I and most of the other programmers in the company were using it instead of Yahoo for search. He told me that it wasn't worth worrying about. Search was only 6% of our traffic, and we were growing at 10% a month. It wasn't worth doing better." David Filo relied on facts to make the wrong prediction. The data was accurate all right, but his interpretation was myopic, and in retrospect, disastrous.

Turning data into useful information is not trivial. It requires experience, care, and often intuition. Simple problems like deciding on the color of a button are reasonably easy to resolve. Run an A/B test, see which color gets a better conversion rate, and go with it. This is true only if you can collect enough data points, of course. Startup companies don't always have this luxury, and their only option is often to JFDI.

When the number of variables increases, it becomes exponentially difficult to draw meaningful conclusions. This is where statistics come into play. Using the right statistical tools for the job is vital. Be careful and know what you're doing; otherwise, your "data-driven management" might devolve into a farce. As John von Neumann put it: "There's no sense in being precise when you don't even know what you're talking about."

Design

The famous architect Eero Saarinen once said: "Always design a thing by considering it in its next larger context - a chair in a room, a room in a house, a house in an environment, and an environment in a city plan." Sage advice for product managers. A product manager works like a designer of products in their larger context, beyond lines of code or plastic molds. Your customer will use your product along with other products and services. It will become part of their lives, integrated into their environment, and consolidated in their ecosystem. Understanding these connections is paramount when designing a winning product.

The only way to fully understand how a product relates to its environment is to put it there and study the outcomes. The lessons learned can then be applied to the next version, which (one would hope) will be better. This examination process should be an integral part of any design process;

designing in a void, with no commercial purpose, may deem you a famous artist but will surely make you a lousy product manager. Observe users to understand their needs by examining and analyzing their usage patterns, and never blindly trust what they say. Making the right product decisions is the primary "artistic" aspect of product management. If you're fortunate enough, you will have enough reliable data to guide you through it.

During World War I, pilots on reconnaissance missions needed to relay information quickly to ground crews. Sending clear voice communication from an open-cockpit biplane is challenging, to say the least, especially with early 20th-century radio and audio technology. Necessity is the mother of invention, and so in 1915, a British team developed an ingenious solution after realizing that ground testing of wind- and noise-resistant microphones was preventing them from reaching a solution. Testing their system in the environment for which it was intended - a windy and noisy cockpit - allowed them to develop a product that was instrumental in winning the war. The team leader, Charles Edmond Prince, later wrote[4]: "it appeared curiously dead and ineffective on the ground, but seemed to take on a new sprightliness in the air."

Stay committed to the long view throughout your product leadership, designing a product that will bring value for many years. As a rule of thumb, design for a younger crowd than what you would naturally do. Young users will be around longer and are more critical in their feedback compared to older ones. By designing for them, you will improve your product's long-term prospects, steering it further toward becoming a platform you and others can build upon.

---

[4] https://spectrum.ieee.org/tech-history/dawn-of-electronics/in-world-war-i-british-biplanes-had-wireless-phones-in-cockpit

As the diagram above shows, human fit, the degree to which the product fits actual customer needs (whether used by humans or not), is no less important than business viability and technical feasibility. Techies and data-minded business people sometimes overlook this fact; it's the product manager's job to act as the voice of the customer and insist that the user is at the top of everybody's mind throughout the entire product life cycle.

The key to creating winning products is to see the forest without losing sight of any tree, flower, or thorn. If you are the only product manager, it all falls on your shoulders. In a team, the top product manager is expected to have the widest angle of view: the coveted 30,000 feet perspective. Other team members are not exempt - they, too, should understand the big picture but are expected to be more intimate with the details of their neck of the woods. This combined wide and narrow angle of view allows them to make the required tradeoffs and take the right path to a winning product design.

Simplicity

"I have written you a long letter because I did not have time to write a short one."
                    - Blaise Pascal

Simplicity is a design philosophy that prefers products leaner on features over ones overloaded with bells and whistles. The key idea is that a simple product done right offers more flexibility and, consequently, more value to the customer. A simple product is more likely to become a platform for user creativity and extensibility simply because the absence of certain features makes this necessary for others to do so. On the business side, the hope is that a more straightforward product will enable upsell and expansion opportunities. Simpler products are also often cheaper to build.

There's something magical about simple products. They allow the customer to focus on the essence with minimal distraction, encouraging deeper engagement. They are often more elegant than their complicated cousins and tend to have a longer lifespan.

As Blaise Pascal noted, getting to Simple is complex. A typical creative process is additive in nature. Stakeholders get attached to the features they have added and find it difficult to let go. Mature products are more likely to become an elaborate hodgepodge of features. Add to that the ubiquitous engineering principle "if it works, don't touch it," and you sometimes end up with an amalgam of old and new features held together with zip ties and duct tape. These situations typically get increasingly messy until someone makes the (long overdue) decision to redesign the product, replace it with a different one, or kill it altogether.

How do you break out of this death spiral? By insisting on simplicity. Simplifying is not free, but it pays off. Ruthlessly cut out the deadwood. Redesign the product to be simpler. Refactor the code to be nimbler. Re-engineer your processes to be more efficient. Be the steward of simplification in your company. True to form, simplify your own (and your team's) habits: write shorter requirements documents, epics, and stories, hold fewer meetings with fewer attendees, and transfer ineffective employees to greener pastures.

Simplification is a constant battle, and too many people succumb to the beast of complexity. If it seems too challenging to beat, it is probably worth the challenge. Don't give up. Insist on Simple.

Capturing Requirements

"Be stubborn on vision but flexible on details."

- Jeff Bezos

The process of capturing requirements and specifying features to build usually starts with articulating use cases. A use case narrative describes how a certain user persona can achieve a goal or solve a problem using your product. Use cases can be turned into a set of specified features. You can also take an intermediary step and define user stories. These typically have a narrower scope than use cases and take the form of "As a <role>, I want to do <task> in order to achieve <goal>."

When the use cases are defined, product managers usually capture the requirement details using one of two methods:

Documents: Marketing Requirements Document (MRD), Product Requirements Document (PRD), or similarly themed documents that describe the market situation and customer use cases and specify the product in varying degrees of detail. When done right, kept up to date, and actually used for implementing the product, these can be a boon for everyone involved. Too often, unfortunately, the effort that goes into writing them is in vain. These documents are associated with the waterfall methodology that has gone by the wayside in the Agile age. They may still be useful for outlining overarching goals and initiatives.

Stories: Agile methodologies like Scrum and Kanban use short, scope-limited feature descriptions (stories) that can be grouped into longer narratives (epics). Long requirements documents are replaced by a list (backlog) of stories or epics, each having one or more acceptance criteria. These are then implemented in priority order in time-bound sprints.

Writing a requirements document is a significant endeavor that can get outpaced by market and technology changes.

The author must keep up with executive decrees, customer demands, and engineering pushbacks. Even after being approved by all stakeholders, these erosive forces might turn it into a voluminous and incoherent collection of details. As a rule of thumb, the longer the document is, the higher the cost of maintaining it. The resulting tome is often untenable and hard to comprehend, and as a result, engineering, QA, and others interpret it as they see fit or ignore it altogether. This defeats the purpose and is one of the driving forces behind the popularity of agile methodologies.

Capturing requirements in stories takes getting used to. Implementing agile methodologies can take a while but is undoubtedly worth it. Some companies adopt a middle-ground approach, writing concise PRDs that consist of epics and short stories. Whatever floats your boat, make sure the requirements you publish:

- Focus on the Why and What, not on the How.

- Are clear and concise.

- Are easy to understand.

- Explain the reasoning behind your decisions.

- Don't sound condescending.

- Provide the right amount of detail.

- Leave room for creative execution.

- Don't specify or suggest an architecture or an implementation method.

The chapter Agile Essence dives deeper into the various aspects of the agile development process.

Prioritizing

"Action expresses priorities."
          - Mahatma Gandhi

Product managers are inundated with feature requests from sales, support, operations, and other sources. Their most important task is deciding which items to handle first, which to take care of later, and which to refuse or ignore altogether. Being able to say no is one of the essential traits of effective product managers, but it's easier said than done for a handful of reasons:

- New ideas tend to look great from 30,000 feet. The ugly truth often reveals itself when you dive into the details: feature conflicts, fierce competition, relying on expensive or theoretical technologies, and on and on. Premature commitments can haunt you for years.

- Many product managers find it difficult to make quick, decisive decisions; this is regretful. Let me put it bluntly: those people should seek other career paths.

- Customers can be very demanding, but you simply can't please all of the people all of the time. Professionals who do that have very different job descriptions.

- Reaching the level of intuitive thinking that makes decision-making easy and natural takes time. It can take you between a few months and a few years to fully understand your product, market, customers, business processes, competition, and all other relevant factors.

No one will congratulate you for wasting resources, so a thorough prioritization process can go a long way toward optimizing resource use. The following tips will help you prioritize more effectively and spend your limited resources on what can make a real difference:

- Break large features into smaller chunks. Do your homework, acquire a deep understanding of everything involved, and decide on the ideal chunk size (we will discuss methods for implementing this later in the book).

- Don't build features too early. If a feature is not necessary now, it may become even more redundant as the product evolves. Only build what you can explain and justify. Don't waste your resources on building features to support your or somebody else's magical thinking.

- The quote "Premature optimization is the root of all evil," attributed to the famed computer scientist Sir Tony Hoare (and popularized by Donald Knuth), applies to most disciplines. In product management terms, don't optimize, redesign, refactor, re-engineer, or re-whatever any product feature unless you have a strong business reason to do so.

Build a Product that People will Buy

"And so castles made of sand
fall into the sea, eventually."
                    - Jimi Hendrix,
            Castles Made Of Sand

Your primary focus should be finding product-market fit and creating a product that people will buy. This applies whether you are running your own company or working for someone else. It's your job #1, regardless of company size or maturity level, across all markets. It's true whether customers buy your product or service directly or indirectly. Forget about the wishful thinking mantra "build it and they will come;" instead, use a fact-based approach that will get people to pay for the product you are building. If your product is part of a broader offering and is provided "for free," make sure it's compelling enough to stand on its own.

When creating a new and innovative product, ensure - as much as you can afford - that people will want to pay for it. In a large company, it's often difficult for a product manager to figure this out, given the layers of separation between them and the customer. If you can't get this information internally, do your own research. Study the technology and the competition, review financial considerations, analyze go-to-market challenges, and explore other relevant factors. Develop your opinion based on as much data as you can put your hands on. Ensure that the product you manage is indeed highly desired by customers (or is extremely likely to be). If you know that the product is going to be a dud, shift your focus. It won't do anyone any good if the product fails, especially you. The earliest you can figure this out, the better, so you can still do something about it.

Pay attention to the difference between "a product that people will want to buy" and "a product that people need." You don't know what people need unless you operate in a mature, high-volume market with a good understanding of the intricate dynamics. Even in that case, predicting what will make people buy your product over your competitors' is challenging. The product they want - or believe they need - depends on many factors at any point in time. You can, for example, try to influence their decision by investing heavily in marketing. This is fine as long as it's part of an overall strategy and not some delusional approach like, "we'll make this mediocre product, sell a ton of it, reinvest the proceeds in advertising, and sell even more!" Yeah, no.

Do

- Study your market and distribution challenges and ensure you understand them thoroughly.

- Test how viable your product is by releasing it as early as possible.

- Iterate and keep improving.

Don't

- Assume you know what customers need.

- Trust customers to be able to articulate their needs.

- Blindly rely on others to tell you what product to build.

Marketing can be costly. Don't pin your hopes on other people's or teams' efforts. Focus instead on building a **product that people will want to buy**. Do your part well, and success will follow, compounded by the actions of others.

The ideal way to find a product that people will want to buy is to iterate. Start by releasing an MVP - a minimum viable product with the most limited feature set anyone would pay for (directly or indirectly through ads or upsells). Ship it and start collecting feedback. Use that feedback and other inputs to decide which features to add or take away. Repeat.

This approach has roots decades ago with products like the airplane, the car, and the mobile phone. They all had their humble beginnings as MVPs and evolved through the combined effort of many companies. Eric Reis' book The Lean Startup covers all aspects of this approach. Reis' definition of "startup" is broad enough to include most entrepreneurial or intrapreneurial endeavors and probably covers yours as well. Steve Blank, author of The Four Steps to the Epiphany, sheds light on the same topic from a process-oriented angle. Both books are well worth your time.

Curating

"Art is making something out of nothing and selling it."
- Frank Zappa

At the top of the long list of terms describing a product manager, there's a deceivingly simple word: Curator. Like a museum curator, a product manager collects outstanding features into an assemblage that exceeds the sum of its parts. Identifying this remarkable combination is, in itself, a work of art. Finding the right product requires a generous helping of creativity, persistence, and attention to detail. A good curator can turn an otherwise bland group of objects into a sellout. Outstanding curation is the epitome of creative product management.

Before starting to put together your show, identify a problem worth solving. What will it focus on? What will make it unique? How many other museums feature similar ones? As you look for a theme, sort through all the data you can put your hands on. You will encounter conflicting information pointing you in different directions and often have to dig deep to find an elusive fact. You will have to learn new concepts and understand multiple disciplines. The more you study your target market and audience, the more clarity you will gain, leading to a better product definition.

With the patience of a Pointillist, put everything together and create a cohesive offering. Not every item can fit in; moreover, the relationship among the ones that make it is crucial. When choosing the features that make up your final product, insist on keeping only the essentials. Each piece of art must have a clear role in the overall makeup of your show. Naturally, you don't want to choose only low-hanging fruit. Favor quality over quantity and ruthlessly throw out features that don't meet your standards. Garbage in, garbage out.

When your masterpiece is ready to be revealed, don't hesitate to open it up to the world. Make an effort to publicize it to ensure that it grows in popularity in its early days until it picks up momentum. In parallel, start planning your next show or expanding the current one to attract a bigger audience. A productive curator never rests.

Part 3

Building and Shipping

The Product Factory

*"Adventure is just bad
planning."*

*- Roald Amundsen,
the first person to reach
the South Pole*

While product managers don't typically build the actual product, they are intimately involved in the process. They maintain a backlog of features that need to be built, evolving based on customer feedback and many other factors. This backlog and the related action plan are then turned into a shippable product by engineering, manufacturing, or service teams, with other groups contributing to the effort.

Creating the product by proxy makes it all the more challenging for product managers. It doesn't get any easier when it comes to shipping and selling it, as this, too, is typically done by others. To be successful, product managers must have a deep understanding of product implementation and sale processes. They ought to be on top of things and ensure that all the auxiliary aspects, like documentation and customer support, are provided on time and with high quality.

In this part of the book, we will explore these elements of product management - those pesky things you need to take care of while the creative phases of identifying and designing the product are well on their way. It would help if you start planning and executing them well in advance rather than treating them as an afterthought. More than any other aspect, these auxiliaries can turn your life into a living hell if not adequately planned for ahead of time.

Backlog Management

"There is nothing quite so useless as doing with great efficiency something that should not be done at all."
— *Peter F. Drucker*

Feature lists, to-do lists, action-item lists, or backlogs: whatever term you use, managing them effectively is an art that takes some time to master. Good product managers are artisans skilled at assembling bits and pieces of information into coherent backlogs that prescribe the creation of winning products.

For greater agility, use a relatively short-term backlog and a longer-term roadmap. The latter is less useful for day-to-day management, as it's not sensitive enough to market and resource fluctuations. Even traditionally conservative markets move quickly; take the car industry, for example. Let's assume you were working for a car manufacturer back in 2000. Would your roadmap include Bluetooth connectivity for mobile phones? Unlikely, as not many people needed that back then. And a more recent example: in 2010, would you build an Android-based dash-mount entertainment system? Probably not. Fast forward another decade, and most new cars support Apple CarPlay and Android Auto. This must have reshuffled roadmaps and displaced other features. A much larger scale example is the transition to electric drivetrains, which is upending the car industry and changing entire product lines.

Backlog changes are fractal in nature. There are long, medium, and short term fluctuations, as demonstrated by the diagram below. The vertical axis represents the degree to which the product matches customer expectations. Each line represents a different aspect, such as price, capabilities, or level of customer support.

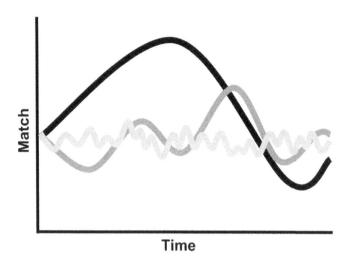

Change happens in multiple time scales

How do you cope with these dynamic patterns and improve your planning? By maintaining a long-term roadmap and a short-term prioritized backlog. The two lists have different levels of accuracy, with the backlog inevitably culled and maintained more frequently.

Building a backlog from scratch (like when planning a new product or a major new addition to an existing one) is difficult but less grueling than ongoing maintenance. The initial roadmap should be lean, defining a feature-limited product that will later grow and develop based on customer feedback. Little is known about the actual requirements at that early stage in the product's life cycle, so it's relatively easy to pick a few features and start there. Use whatever data you can obtain and make the best decision you can afford to make. Regardless, you will have to make significant changes later on.

Backlogs need periodic TLC. Rates of change and implementation velocities vary, so the review frequency can change from daily to weekly to monthly. When reviewing, be critical and eliminate any features that are no longer necessary. Modify the rest based on what you have learned since the previous review. A typical review cycle will use the following criteria and reasoning:

Short Term	Medium Term	Long Term
React to immediate customer needs	Evolve product features in response to customer feedback	Anticipate market trends and technological advancements

As dull and tedious as the review process may be, don't let the backlog go unattended for too long. It can quickly turn into a scattered list of features that don't look familiar or important anymore. Be efficient and keep the list clean and up to date. Do this repeatedly, and you will reap the benefits throughout the life of the product.

Dependencies

*"Freedom is not worth having
if it does not include the
freedom to make mistakes."*
                - Mahatma Gandhi

Reducing dependencies - ideally removing them - is crucial for creating winning products. The more elements you keep under your control, the more flexibility you can afford. Conversely, the more you depend on certain resources, the more painful it becomes when they don't meet your expectations. Software libraries, hardware platforms, key engineers, and consultants with specific expertise may all be necessary but can become a liability if you depend on them blindly. As much as you can affect it, don't bet your product's future on somebody else's technology or capabilities. Having said that, I'm all for outsourcing and reaping the benefit of moving forward faster. Deciding which elements to farm out and which to keep in-house is a challenge. As a rule of thumb, keep the core development close to your chest and consider outsourcing the peripherals. Here are a few examples of dependencies that are safer to rely on:

- A patent licensed for a very long term.

- An open-source library that can be easily swapped out if it fails to deliver.

- A team member that has a significant vested interest in the company's success.

- A CPU expected to remain sufficiently powerful for the life of the product.

- An outsourced team working on non-critical parts

Making "build vs. buy" decisions (or, more accurately, "build, buy, or partner") is becoming more common as more and more services become available. Some notable examples include cloud hosting, authentication services, payment processing, financial account aggregation, and a seemingly endless number of open-source libraries. In reality, there are a few options when planning and implementing new features:

- Build it yourself, possibly reinventing the wheel
- License or buy somebody else's product and integrate it with yours
- Use an open-source alternative

- Partner with another company that will take care of this capability
- Some combination of the above options

At a startup company, you can't afford to build everything yourself. In fact, you can often afford to buy or build only the bare minimum before securing more funding. Large companies, on the other hand, tend to make more stuff themselves. At the end of the spectrum, for example, are companies that design the chips they use, notably Apple, Alphabet (Google), Meta (Facebook), Amazon, and Microsoft. You have to reach mega scale before it makes financial sense to design your own silicon. Achieving vertical integration and building almost everything yourself allows you to tightly integrate hardware and software into one consistent product offering with superb user experience, so it makes sense if your scale and resources enable it.

A practical approach for smaller companies deciding which dependencies to keep is to list those you have absolutely no choice but to develop in-house and those you could potentially replace or remove. All items on the latter list must be justified before investing in them any further. Review the lists periodically, and don't blindly assume that past decisions were correct; conditions change and requirements evolve, so what was once right might cost you dearly now or in the future.

Be aware that shifting tasks and resources around involves considerable switching costs. The only way to avoid bad decisions is to do your homework and understand the tradeoffs involved.

Estimating

"Everything that can be counted does not necessarily count; everything that counts cannot necessarily be counted."
- Albert Einstein

Product managers should have a good understanding of everything it takes to build and ship their products. Most of all, they must understand the capacity and expected velocity of the human resources involved. While the work itself is beyond their direct control, being able to estimate how long the job will take is extremely helpful when working with engineering managers and others.

Estimating time and resources is notoriously difficult. Errors are proportional to the size of the project; the larger the project, the further off your estimate will be. Getting it wrong by 50 or 100 percent is not uncommon. Even experienced product and project managers often make these mistakes, yet they are still expected to deliver estimates that will aid in resource planning.

When it comes to estimating completion times, many people tend to fall into one of two camps:

Under-estimators: Overly optimistic and tend to have a firm conviction in their ability to finish on time. These folks often ignore team dynamics and outside pressures, overlook feature creep, and discount technological barriers. They tend to miss the big picture and provide lowball estimates. Worse still, they don't seem to learn from their mistakes. A sub-group, having learned its lesson, refuses to estimate altogether or insists on providing only ballpark estimates.

Over-estimators: Some would call them pessimistic, but they prefer "realistic." They are either incapable of estimating or tend to sandbag their estimates to relieve the pressure they experience. Their time estimates are way off on the high side, leading to messed-up sales projections (too low) and chaotic resource management ("We are done, now what?").

The best antidote for the estimation challenge is to divide and conquer. While it doesn't guarantee success, it certainly increases the likelihood. It's easier to estimate the magnitude of small tasks. The process of adding them up gives you another opportunity to reevaluate the project at large. Product managers are often "the adult in the room," insisting on making a data-driven decision (if at all possible) and helping the team converge on the most reasonable estimate.

When budgeting, managers tend to be creative with their estimates. No one wants their next year's budget cut, so they try to justify this year's resource use by inflating their estimates. Their managers are aware of that, of course; after all, they were in those shoes only a few years back. A cat-and-mouse game ensues.

When data is unavailable, estimates become guesstimates. In many cases, the published estimate results from compromise, leaving all sides somewhat dissatisfied. It's not uncommon for the higher-ranking manager to force an unrealistic estimate in order to prove their point and solidify authority. Here, everybody loses unless the company's fortune changes consistent with that estimate, making the boss look prescient. Lucky bastard.

Project Management

When it comes to getting things done, a product manager is like a film producer. Project management is often considered one of the less attractive aspects of product management. Unlike that producer, you typically don't stand to gain a massive cash fallout even if your product becomes a smash hit. Production consists of a whole lot of administrivia. Even after you automate or farm out the easy parts, there remain plenty of tasks for you to do day in and day out. Whichever project management tool you end up using, you're still going to do plenty of clerical work, which may include:

- Making sure people have the resources they need to get things done.

- Reminding people about pending milestones and ensuring they are on track to achieving them.

- Writing progress reports at various levels of detail.

- Scheduling meetings.

- Rescheduling because Joe just found out that he has a conflict.

- Rescheduling again because Quality couldn't finish testing on time, and you run the risk of a deadline slippage.

- Rescheduling yet again because engineering ran into a new snag, and the beta release won't be ready on time.

- And so on...

Countless books have been written on project management, and about the same number of theories and methods have been devised to try and improve it. I'm a fan of agile methodologies, but to each their own. Use whatever method works for you; just keep an eye open to new ideas and experiment with unfamiliar ones. Don't make the mistake of latching on to one method and applying it to every scenario.

Even if you don't use agile project management, borrow at least one page from the agile playbook: opt for small tasks rather than large ones. Small tasks are easier to estimate, allocate, and shuffle around. If they need to be delayed or canceled for any reason, it's less likely to cause significant repercussions. You have more flexibility in reassigning or modifying them without provoking excessive pushback. In short, they make your life easier.

Agile Essence

"Life is what happens to you while you're busy making other plans."

- John Lennon

Agile methodologies have been trending up and down (but mostly up) in the last two decades. Agile is no longer for software development only; creative teams "go agile" in businesses ranging from graphic design to semiconductor engineering. Agile processes work well if you keep a critical principle in mind, conspicuously missing from the Agile Manifesto[5]: **Don't waste time**. The ultimate goal of implementing any business process is increasing efficiency in terms of time and resources. What you spend time on is the most significant variable you can control in a team with fixed resources.

---

[5] http://agilemanifesto.org

I believe in optimizing for the outcome, not the process, and I am skeptical of any prescribed technique. Agile is "for the people, by the people." As such, the people (engineers, in most cases) should have the last word on how the process works:

Sprints: how long should the sprints be? Should they all have the same length and purpose? Should they even be time-bounded?

Estimations: how to estimate task sizes? Points (and if so, how much is one point), hours, days, or no estimates at all?

Meetings: how often should the team meet? What structure will meetings have, if any?

Scrum master: are they necessary?

Product owner: are they a product manager? An engineer? Or maybe a QA person? The notion that only product managers represent the voice of the customer is overrated. Everybody can (and should) do it. Then again, business decisions – in this context – are the product manager's to make.

The goal is not to please the "agile gods" by following a rigid set of rules. The goal is to move faster and more efficiently, ultimately creating a more profitable product. You can't do this by sticking to some "best practices" outlined in some book or a blog post (including this one). It can only be done through a candid discussion with the team to hash out the options and find a methodology that works best for everyone. The process should then be optimized until no more inefficiency can be squeezed out of it, with one primary goal in mind: don't waste time!

Quality

"Real quality must be the source of the subjects and objects."

> *- Robert M. Pirsig,*
> *Zen and the Art of*
> *Motorcycle Maintenance*

Quality is hard to define, but you know it when you see it. While optimizing product features based on utility and cost, quality is often sacrificed, being too expensive to maintain. For the customer, perceived quality comes from the sum total of their experience. For example, an inferior product can still be considered high quality when accompanied by stellar customer service. Robert M. Pirsig wouldn't have approved of that, but this is a market reality.

Assuming you do what most ethical companies do - relying on the quality of the product itself to boost your overall score - you are not likely to produce a very high-quality product at first. It simply doesn't make business sense. Instead, start with the highest quality you can afford (read: that your customers can afford) and iterate in successive product versions in an attempt to increase the overall perceived quality.

Feedback drives quality up, to a degree

The more feedback you collect and use to improve the product, the better it becomes. At some point, however, product quality plateaus, and no amount of additional feedback can improve it significantly.

When your product reaches this level of maturity, you should be far into the next generation's life cycle.

Successive generations, when done right, increase perceived quality. Typically, though, the marginal benefit decreases with each generation. It's rare to find a late-generation product that is drastically better than the preceding one.

Subsequent generations increase quality, with a decreasing benefit

Sometimes, the next generation is a [relative] failure, applying downward pressure on the perceived quality. This may happen when betting on an unproven technology or taking other uncalculated risks. It can be a good motivator for re-engineering the product and re-energizing the team with the promise of bringing back the fame and fortune you once enjoyed. Often, however, it's a sign that your multi-generational product is reaching the end of its useful life.

Productizing

Ideas and concepts become actual products only when accompanied by an array of supporting elements: documentation, spare parts, technical support, integration, customization, and more. While other stakeholders typically provide most of these, it's ultimately up to the product manager to see that they are indeed delivered as planned and at a level commensurate with the product itself.

Productization is the process of transforming a working gizmo into a product that customers would want to buy. Some product managers find it difficult to accept the fact that the whole productization gamut is within their realm of responsibility. It's a lot to think of, and the tendency is to ignore it in hopes that others will take care of it. Big mistake.

Don't bet your product's future (and yours) on other people's good intentions. Start by understanding all productization aspects. Making a list can help; mark the owner next to each item, realizing that you're the CEO of your product hence ultimately responsible for everything.

Your list should encompass the entire offering - a product package you feel comfortable with, one that allows you to position the product competitively from a cost/benefit angle. And it wouldn't be complete without sales collateral and support infrastructure.

In fact, post-sale support is one of the most frequently neglected elements of productization. Providing best-of-class customer support and professional services (if applicable) is crucial for building long-term customer relationships, increasing retention, and spurring repeat sales and upgrades. Even if your industry's standard practice is not to provide any, you can outdo the competition by exceeding your customers' expectations. Every product should include a good user manual or an instruction set built into the product itself. You can do even better: design a product that does not need any instructions. This will not eliminate the need to provide customer service in most cases; however, a more straightforward product will require less of it.

Publishing a Roadmap

*"An orgasm is the benefit.
The vibrator is just a feature"*
               - Anonymous

Good roadmaps are clear and concise. Better roadmaps are - on top of that - always kept up to date, which is more demanding than it sounds. The best roadmaps are clear and concise, up-to-date, and correct. How can you test a roadmap's correctness? by comparing it with reality. You're doing well if it's more than 80% accurate. That's a good heuristic for old roadmaps, but what about the one you're working on right now? Since you can't predict the future, every roadmap you put out is based on best-effort prognostication, and the pressures you're under affect its level of detail, granularity, clarity, and correctness.

Everyone everywhere is always asking for a detailed roadmap, and they all have great reasons for having one:

- Salespeople, so they can sell the future (and sometimes make dubious commitments on your behalf).

- Marketing folks, so they can plan launch activities and announce upcoming features

- Engineering teams, so they can staff at the right level ahead of time.

- Executive management, so they can scrutinize the product strategy and include it in presentations and reports.

Your interest, however, is not to publish a roadmap at all, thereby reducing dependencies and allowing for maximal flexibility. This is not realistic, of course, so you must decide on the level of granularity in terms of features and time periods. You can choose any point on the graph below; granularity varies depending on the industry, type of product, competitive pressures, and other factors. The middle is a good compromise if you are working on a B2B product, as it usually quenches the thirst for roadmap details and keeps a reasonable degree of flexibility.

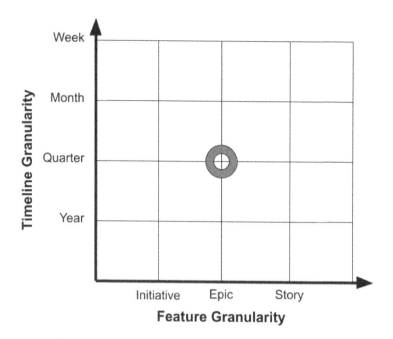

Roadmap granularity is defined by timeline resolution and the level of detail in feature descriptions

Features and Benefits

Confusing features and benefits can easily derail an otherwise great roadmap. It muddles the message and makes it difficult to follow. Let's start with the basic definitions:

Benefits are what the customers care about. Benefits usually have an emotional or financial value and improve the customer's life.

Features are what engineering teams care about. They are usually technical in nature. Keep feature descriptions lean on implementation details to increase the chance of getting them right.

Here's a recipe for constructing roadmap items, helping keep it clear and concise by placing each benefit and feature pair in one sentence. The roadmap is essentially a list of these pairs, organized on a timeline. Each roadmap item should have this format:

<benefit> <preposition> *<feature>*

The preposition, e.g., "by" or "through," can be substituted for an expression like "using," "leveraging," "owing to," "enabled by," "improved by," "mitigated by," "powered by," "generated by," or "secured by." For example:

- **Accurate sleep tracking** powered by *an under-pillow sensor*

- **Super fast loading** enabled by *a high-speed network interface*

- **Zero punctures** by using *airless tires*

- **Fast emoji selection** through *a dedicated emoji keyboard*

- **Bursts of pleasurable flavor** emanating from *caramel swirls*

In summary, when creating a roadmap, consider the following:

Time horizon: The shorter it is, the easier it will be to change direction if necessary. You can't predict the future; things will change regardless of your best intentions.

Level of detail: the fewer details you include, the more likely you are to get it right - not because you or your engineering team are clueless, but because things will inevitably change. You can't un-send a roadmap to a customer.

Granularity: the less granular it is, the easier it will be to tweak implementation details to fit evolving market needs and product architecture changes.

Commercializing

"Profit = Revenue - Cost"
- Business 101

The formula in the quote above summarizes two years of business school. There are two ways to maximize profit. The formula illuminates them both and illustrates what product managers should do: strive to maximize revenue while minimizing cost in order to generate profit. It's really that simple in theory, but making it happen is a different story.

Minimizing cost is an essential business dictum. Product managers do their part by defining products that require the least amount of resources to build and maintain. Wasteful products are bound to fail sooner or later, and you can help avoid that fate by making them leaner and meaner as early as possible. The longer you wait, the more technical debt you accumulate and the harder it is to dig your way out of it. It's always possible to redesign or re-engineer, but if you don't do it early enough, you will end up with no product to optimize.

From a product management perspective, maximizing revenue requires taking the sales aspects into account from the onset of the product definition process. As a product manager, you must understand how your product will be sold, through which channels, and at what price points. You need to understand the competition and its offering, as well as your and other companies' complementary products.

Ideally, it would help if you determine the pricing strategy or at least have a say in it. While pricing theory is beyond the scope of this book, here are two examples that illustrate the importance of making product-aware pricing decisions:

Disguised money-making features: Apple makes certain iPhone models available at different price points, and virtually the only difference is the amount of storage available. The perceived difference is enormous, though, as evident by the fact that consumers pay upward of $200 for a 256GB increase in memory capacity. The steadily decreasing cost of those extra 256GB is in the sub $10 range. Apple makes a cool $190 on each higher-end model sold, on top of the base profit. Not bad. This is enabled by the fact that, lacking a memory expansion slot, you can't add storage capacity post-purchase. Your only option is to buy a model with more memory, and Apple is nice enough to point out how much memory your photos and videos will require in a subtle effort to nudge you toward a higher price. This is a classic example of how a product feature, seemingly designed to simplify the product, is actually meant to drive up profit.

Anchoring: The Relativity Trap or Anchoring Effect describes our tendency to make comparative rather than absolute decisions. It's easier to choose from a small set of items by comparing them to each other. It works to our benefit most of the time, but not always. A good example is food pricing. Restaurants often have a menu item they don't expect anyone to order. It often has a sophisticated-sounding name like Steak Flambé Parisien, and always comes with a hefty price tag. They put it on the menu for one reason: to shift the frame of reference upwards. The unsuspecting diner compares a low-priced item, a mid-tier one, and that French delicacy that goes for $89.95 apiece and opts for the middle option. Lacking that high-priced anchor, they will go for low-end items more often than not, so it's a no-brainer for restaurant managers to use this trick. The same concept is employed in a variety of markets. Keep it in mind at your next pricing meeting.

Shipping

When the product and its peripherals are ready, it's time to get it out the door. This may not be as easy as it seems. Companies find plenty of excuses to delay product releases. The primary concern is that the product is not ready for prime time. Guess what: if you don't expose it to real users, it will never be. With new versions of existing products, pushback usually sounds like this: "Customers won't like it," "The new version is not differentiated enough," or conversely, "it's too much of a departure from the existing one." The argument is similar when dealing with new products: "Customers won't like it. It's not differentiated enough from the competition," or "it is so different that it's going to fail." The common claim is that "a little more time" is needed to perfect the product and get it ready. This often leads to a ceaseless feature creep that ends in a deadline squeeze. The result is a bloated product with features most customers don't need.

Many factors lead product managers to hesitate before pushing the "Ship" button. Steve Jobs famously stated: "real artists ship," and this from a man who was the consummate perfectionist. If he could ship anything, so can mere mortals like you and me. So, what stands in our way? Fear. Fear for our company, for our job, and for our future. Nobody wants to be associated with a flop.

Releasing your product is much like letting your child go their own way. Don't let separation anxiety paralyze you. Teach them to be independent throughout their upbringing. Many of the actions you take as a parent seem unrelated, but at the end of the day, most of them are geared toward fostering successful independence, making your kids the pride of your later years. Same with products; your real goal should be to let go and have the product support itself, becoming the shining star of your P&L.

Luckily for us product managers, technology makes it increasingly easier to make the fear go away. Cloud software provides the luxury of continuous, selective deployment of incremental versions to a subset of users. If anything goes wrong, you can roll back, fix, and try again. Not all products make a natural fit for continuous deployment - for example, those with strict regulatory compliance requirements. With the benefits of cloud software solidifying, companies find creative solutions in these cases as well.

Some suggest turning fear of shipping into fear of not shipping[6]. Brilliant idea! Product managers determine what product to build and facilitate the building process. Shipping should be an integral part of their job description, and fear of not shipping should be their primary concern.

Building a Sellable Product

"Job titles don't matter.
Everyone is in sales. It's the
only way we stay in business."
        - Harvey Mackay

Everybody, not just salespeople, is in the business of moving people to act. Product managers are a prime example, of course. While they don't close deals directly, their most significant contribution to sales is creating products that sell themselves - products that are so desirable that demand generation is not required, and people stand in line to get

---

[6] https://joel.is/fear-of-not-shipping

one. While this is a worthy goal, it's rarely achieved and seldom sustained.

Some of your actions as a product manager can make this a reality, while others can stifle it. Here are some ideas for building inherently sellable products that can sustain (and grow!) a self-perpetuating business:

- Don't skimp on quality. Intrinsic quality is one of the best investments in igniting a word-of-mouth wildfire.

- Build viral features that make the product sticky, features that make it sell itself. A classic example: Hotmail, one of the first web-based email services, became super popular by mentioning itself at the bottom of every email sent. Recipients, even those who had never heard of Hotmail, were offered a free account. This is the norm nowadays and email is free for all, but it was pretty innovative back when Hotmail started.

- Add collaboration features, even to seemingly asocial products. For example, enterprise software companies are gradually adding features like chat and gamification, recognizing that enterprise applications should be more fun to use. These applications, boring as they may be, can become more user-friendly when users are allowed to share and engage with their peers. This makes them stickier and wins free advocates.

- Growth hackers are essentially product managers focused on growing the available market, either by finding more opportunities within the natural market or by expanding beyond its boundaries. They can be particularly effective in saturated, commoditized, or otherwise highly competitive markets. The mere fact that someone makes an effort to define, measure, and target these previously uncharted territories increases the likelihood of monetizing them. If successful, the increased market share will give your product more mindshare and get it closer to becoming the market leader.

In your quest to build that coveted self-promoting product, avoid these pitfalls:

- Blindly believing your own messaging: "We have these couple of features, and they are so awesome. Once people realize that, we will surely win them over. I know what the problem is - our marketing strategy sucks!" Not so fast. If your product were genuinely fantastic, it would sell like hotcakes, and you wouldn't even have to think about marketing.

- Ignoring the data: if studying market and customer feedback doesn't lead to a course of action, get more data. Don't ignore inconclusive evidence just because you're too lazy to corroborate it.

- Do not patronize your future, current, or previous customers. Don't indoctrinate them or pretend you're smarter than they are. Be humble, human, and honest. The same goes for competitors. Win because of who you are and what your product is, not because of what others are not.

Part 4

Strategizing, Marketing, and Selling

Strategy

"Take your time, think a lot
Think of everything
you've got
For you will still be here
tomorrow
But your dreams may not"
- Cat Stevens / Yusuf Islam,
Father And Son

The word strategy is often misused and sometimes abused. People invoke it to justify inaction ("first, let's come up with a strategy") or rationalize poor execution ("our strategy was to ship fast and iterate!"). While important, strategy alone does not a product make; success requires stellar execution.

The overarching term "Strategy" can be divided into three elements that should be clearly articulated, kept up to date, and published for all product builders, marketers, and sellers to see:

Mission statement: a set of guiding principles, long-term goals, or a north star for the business. For example: "develop a fully autonomous self-driving car."

Long-term strategy: a plan of action, typically with a one to three-year time horizon. For example: "develop a self-driving car that can navigate the streets of San Francisco with a safety driver at the wheel."

Short-term strategy: a near-term roadmap, typically spanning the next few quarters. For example: "sign a partnership agreement with a major car manufacturer and integrate our self-driving technology into their platform."

The three elements are nested: short-term strategy is defined within the scope of the long-term strategy, which is defined within the outline of the mission statement. If the inner elements spill over their boundary, it's time to review all three and adjust them to match reality.

The three elements that make up a strategy

The mission statement is created at the executive or even board level. A long-term strategy is devised by the highest levels of the product, marketing, sales, operations, engineering, and other teams and must be coordinated with and approved by executive management. Product and engineering teams - and other relevant stakeholders - typically define a short-term strategy and execute it.

Some companies come up with grandiose mission statements, followed by unattainable strategies. You typically hear about the ones that lucked out and became unicorns, but the vast majority fade away and out of memory. At these companies, strategy proclamations are often followed by unrealistic execution plans detached from reality. When this happens, the downstream effect can be depressing for product management and fatal for the company at large. Big bets are important, and a few of them work out well. As a product leader, you can improve outcomes by helping the company make realistic plans.

Ideally, the strategy should lead execution by a healthy margin. This is the textbook situation where the executive team sets a clear direction followed closely by detailed tactical plans and effective execution. When things get out of hand, however, companies find themselves in one of two extremes:

- Strategy lags behind execution (often euphemized as engineering-led innovation) where executives don't measure up to engineering leadership and the product team charts new territory, pretty much ignoring executive-sanctioned strategy.
- Strategy is way ahead of execution: this is the other extreme, often caused by a delusional megalomaniac at the helm setting unattainable goals. A runaway strategy can also result from a major rift between the executive and product/engineering sides of the house.

In many cases, product managers don't have a say about the mission statement or strategy. Their role is limited to executing to the best of their ability. If you strongly disagree with your company's strategy, ask questions and try to induce change. Arguing with higher-ups over and over again may be counterproductive, however. If you feel that your voice is not being heard, it may be time to move on and join a company where you can take a more active part in strategy formulation.

Competitive Threats

"When you continuously compete with others you become bitter, but when you continuously compete with yourself you become better."
- Marie Blanchard

One of your tasks as a product manager is gathering accurate and detailed competitive information and keeping it up to date. This entails following competitor announcements, tracking media mentions, reading analyst reports, talking to customers and prospects about the products they're using or considering, and gathering competitive intelligence covertly. It helps if you organize the information meticulously in a spreadsheet or a database of some sort, making it easy to find, correlate, and cross-reference competitive data. Maintaining such a database can help you be proactive as you create your roadmap. The more you learn about the market and its actors, the more accurate your predictions will be. Your goal is to predict your competitors' moves and preempt them by building features and launching them first.

There are all sorts of ways to react to competitive threats. Some people get distracted and give their competitors more attention than they warrant. Others act nonchalantly and pretend they couldn't care less. Direct competitive threats can be terrifying. One of the most alarming scenarios is discovering a competing product from a more established company that essentially replicates what you've been working on for a couple of years. This can sap your energy and drain the team's morale. Depending on the timing and intensity of the threat, competitors can hamper your efforts before you have time to respond, gaining market share and mindshare and leaving you in the dust.

The default approach is to identify the competitive gaps and close them as fast as possible. Ideally, your product would leapfrog the alternatives and exceed customer expectations. This is easy in theory but harder in practice. Another approach for dealing with a competitive situation is to reach out to the competitor and see if you can collaborate or at least agree on a "no hostility" relationship based on territory or market segment. These agreements tend to fall apart soon enough when one of the parties steps into the other's turf despite the peace accord.

Closing the competitive gaps is the default approach for a good reason: you usually have no other option. One of your superiors will freak out sooner or later, dreading their quota evaporating or their stock options turning into worthless pieces of paper and demanding that you "do something about it." If the gaps are manageable, by all means, close them. Otherwise, "doing something about it" can be tricky. If you find yourself in this situation, you probably could have done a better job avoiding it in the first place.

Panic is counterproductive. It's better to react rationally and offer a measured response aimed at re-positioning your product and making it more attractive than your competitors'. Ideally, you'd be de-positioning their product at the same time. This may entail reshuffling your roadmap, working with the engineering team to build new features in short order, helping the marketing team create battle cards, presenting the latest threats to the sales team, and calming everyone down - especially the doomsday prognosticators.

Competitive threats come and go; markets are dynamic, and companies constantly change course and refocus. Instead of panicking when a new competitive threat comes into the scene, plan and execute a well-thought-of response that will take the sting out and render it harmless. This will demonstrate your ability to command the situation and position you as an effective product leader.

Positioning

Positioning is the subtle art of setting your product up for success. Your product can do many things for many people; the team worked day and night to perfect it and add all the bells and whistles you specified. In a perfect world, customers will eagerly await all these features after getting drunk on your marketing slogans. When the product is finally launched, hordes of anxious users will flock in from all over the place and use every amazing feature you have built. They will get to know the product better than you and find every obscure feature endlessly useful.

Since this fantasy is not going to materialize anytime soon, you must position your product correctly and sharpen your messaging to ensure that it resonates with the target audience.

One of the most significant decisions is how broad your target market is. The narrower it is, the more targeted the messaging can be. Most companies play in established categories or sub-categories. These categories are typically defined by industry analysts and gradually gain broader acceptance. If no category exists, you can create one. If you're successful, you could win big. Some examples that come to mind are Uber leading the creation of the ride-share category and Apple leading the creation of the smartphone category. For startup companies, category creation is a high-risk move with a huge potential upside. It typically requires a significant investment in thought leadership, which product management can contribute to by participating in messaging efforts, writing articles, creating trade show demos, speaking at conferences, and more.

Your target audience is a subset of all people who may want to buy your product. Targeting is a bit like gerrymandering, a process in which politicians manipulate electoral district boundaries in order to achieve favorable outcomes. While gerrymandering has negative and unethical connotations, voting districts are often adjusted for good reasons, like increasing demographic equality. Regardless, you get to choose your customers, much like politicians "choose their voters." When tweaking the characteristics of your target segment(s) to maximize profit, you want to target those parts of the total available market that need it the most and can afford it.

Furthermore, they should be able to deploy it, use it, benefit from it, and tell their friends about it. Finding that segment (or segments) is an ongoing pursuit that will keep you busy throughout the life of the product. In fact, you will likely end up targeting multiple segments or verticals, for example, various industries, company sizes, and geographies. For each segment, you may need different targeted messaging.

Before creating your messaging, you need to position your product correctly, so it becomes more attractive to the target audience than competing products. Determining the ideal market segments to target will allow you to tweak your product to fit these segments better. You can do this by first gaining a deep understanding of the target segments and their associated ecosystems. Next, you can develop a series of statements describing the features and benefits customers in these segments care about the most.

Work with a team of stakeholders (e.g., product marketing, sales, customer success) to zero in on the ones that resonate most with customers. The goal is to whittle down the list of benefits until you end up with about three to five primary ones. These can be the basis of your positioning statements, describing your target market and how you plan to win with your product.

Positioning is like carefully aiming a pool cue before hitting the cue ball. It's critical to understand the position of all the balls on the pool table and, only then, strike at the right angle and intensity. That planning-before-executing stage is crucial because once you make your move, it's too late to correct it. Stretching the pool metaphor a bit further: as you learn more about the characteristics of the table, the cue, and the balls, you can adjust your aim in the following rounds. With business positioning, you should study the outcomes of your positioning efforts and adjust the messaging, roadmap, and marketing campaigns to better target the market. Once every so often, you want to review and recalibrate your positioning to ensure it remains ahead of the market.

Messaging

"If you don't give the market the story to talk about, they'll define your brand's story for you."

- David Brier

Companies create messaging around various topics. At the top level, they create a story about the company itself, typically painting it as influential and innovative yet trustworthy and ethical. This core image is projected through all communication channels: corporate website, advertising campaigns, tradeshows, and of course, the products and services themselves.

While product managers may get involved in such high-level messaging initiatives, especially at smaller companies, they are more likely to be asked to contribute to product-specific messaging. These efforts revolve around the company's product, product lines, and services. Telling a compelling product story is an effective way to get people to want to use and ultimately buy your product.

Crafting a good story is an art more than a science. In a corporate setting, the story is subject to internal and external pressures and must be constantly adapted. It's not enough to spend a month or two creating a story depicting your product as the ultimate option in your category. Markets and trends shift quickly; no matter how special and unique your story is, it will eventually become yesterday's news. Your story must evolve in order to remain relevant.

The target audience for your story is your potential customer base. It also includes existing customers (targeting renewals and upsells), partners, investors, potential employees, and current ones. As a consumer of stories, you know how important it is for the story to speak to your sensibilities.

Reading a book written for a different audience or watching a movie made for a taste other than yours can be tedious and annoying. Your product's story must therefore resonate well with all potential audiences.

The challenge is compounded by the fact that companies oftentimes target different subcategories. For example, you may serve customers in the construction, transportation, healthcare, and financial services industries. The same message is not going to work for all of them. You will need to craft the master story, then split it into vertical-specific stories that cover their unique use cases and target their specific user personas, for example, by mentioning titles and roles from that particular industry. Using industry-specific terms and relating to the business goals they care about will make your target audience feel you understand their issues and can solve them. All and all, it will make your story much more relatable.

Unfortunately, it is too common for companies to tell a generic story in an effort to please everyone. The result is usually some generic platitude that pleases pretty much nobody, like "Our innovative product leverages advanced technologies to achieve groundbreaking results." It sounds impressive, but it describes pretty much all competitors and countless other companies. Don't fall into this trap. Make a sincere effort to tell category-specific and vertical-specific stories that your customers and target audience can easily relate to.

The marketing team typically owns messaging. However, product managers should be involved in the effort. If you are asked to contribute, accept the invitation. Otherwise, try to insert yourself into this process. You want to be part of it so you can be the voice of truth in this effort. With all their good intentions, marketing folks tend to tell fantastic tales with a loose grasp of reality. Your role is to help them tell a credible story. It doesn't have to be 100% accurate (it's marketing, after all), but it must be backed by facts.

Incorrect messaging can easily backfire. A customer will read about your solution and how it can solve their problem and sign up for a free trial or ask for a demo. This is very exciting! The customer is hopeful, the sales team is happy to get an inbound lead, and everyone expects this to end well. As the sales process progresses, it eventually leads to tough questions about promises made in your marketing collateral. Since the sales team doesn't know the answer, they'll offer a follow-up call with a product manager. What started as a very optimistic story morphed into a firefighting drill that just landed on your desk. Walking back unrealistic expectations hyped up by an adventurous marketing team is now your headache.

If you find yourself in this situation, you have failed to proactively plug yourself into the messaging effort that started months or even years earlier. This kind of customer call can be extremely embarrassing, requiring you to back-paddle in real time. It often ends in failure business-wise, and you may also take a personal hit. At worst, you will be considered a liar by the customer, who will move on and seek other solutions. Internally, you'll be viewed as a naysayer and a pessimist for spoiling a promising sales opportunity.

Get to know the marketing and messaging folks, build rapport, and earn their trust. You want to be part of the ideation and creation process from the get-go instead of reviewing the results late in the process when the team is already set in its ways. By then, you may be unable to squash any false narratives they spun up. Instead, they may think you are crying wolf and find ways to ignore your feedback.

Generating Demand

"If people like you, they'll listen to you, but if they trust you, they'll do business with you."
                    - Zig Ziglar

As a product manager, your focus is on defining and building the right product, not marketing and demand generation. You also typically don't own product or technical marketing, though you will likely work closely with the people in these roles. What can you do to help generate demand and inbound leads? The answer is to build the best product possible - a product that will sell itself. This entails all aspects of a good product. Imagine a latest-model mobile phone. It's smooth. It's slick. It's beautiful. It's powerful. It's fast. It's fully capable. It's versatile. It just works. Oh, and it's addictive. While this might be impossible to achieve in the first ten or so versions of your product, these are good goals to aspire to.

How do you achieve this? by relentlessly pursuing excellence and putting yourself into users' and buyers' shoes: studying the market, tracking usage patterns, and collecting (and implementing!) customer feedback. It boils down to doing what you're supposed to be doing as a product manager: creating the best product possible. In other words, your contribution to demand generation is to do your damn job and do it well. The product itself then becomes a demand generation machine, driving new and repeat sales.

Product-led growth is an increasingly popular approach that embodies this sentiment. Several popular products, like HubSpot, Zoom, and Slack, use this strategy, putting the product itself out front and using it as the primary marketing tool. When it works, you hardly need to invest in sales, relatively speaking. When it comes to B2B productivity tools, the idea is to create a service that is so useful and fun to use that users will adopt it even if Corporate IT doesn't sanction it. As these new tools grow in popularity and demand increases organically, they reach the point of no return, forcing the organization to adopt them officially.

Another way product managers can help generate demand is by creating unique content that will rank high in search engines or otherwise gain popularity. This may include blog posts, technical marketing documents, datasheets, whitepapers, etc. You can also help by encouraging engineers and other stakeholders to generate content by allocating time for them to do so. Putting it on their sprint backlogs will ensure they don't stretch themselves too thin and achieve better results.

Another way to contribute is by participating in conferences: speaking, presenting, networking, and staffing your company's booth. While this is often an integral part of a product manager's job, the amount of preparation and attention you devote to it will significantly affect its effectiveness. Getting engineers in front of customers is a great way to get them motivated and an excellent way to gather user feedback in an unmitigated way. Allocating time for them to get in front of customers will surely make it more enjoyable and effective.

Many product managers become brand advocates and take part in paid marketing activities. Their presentations and product demonstrations are more impactful when they demonstrate market and product mastery. If this is your goal, start by getting yourself out there and doing "volunteer work" for the marketing group; if you're good at attracting an audience, they'll surely want you back as the star of the show.

Customer Acquisition

"Don't find customers for your products, find products for your customers."

- Seth Godin

Acquiring new customers is obviously critical for any business. While sales and business development teams own this task and carry the quota, others, like product managers, are often called upon for assistance. It's essential to understand the customer's buying process in order to reduce purchasing friction. An enterprise customer may take your company and your product through several approval steps, including:

- Competitive analysis to explore alternative options
- Business unit review to reaffirm the need
- Vendor qualification and approval
- Contract review
- Security review
- Purchasing committee approval
- Multiple levels of executive approval

Each one of these steps can take weeks to complete. Added up, the process can easily take years. While the sales team can skillfully navigate this process, as a product manager, you can help by building features to help remove friction from the purchasing and renewal processes. For example:

- Role-based access controls for streamlined approval and renewal

- Dashboards that display usage clearly and can help justify an upsell

- Friendly renewal reminders that prompt the customer to take action in a timely manner

- A grace period to allow them to continue using the product for a while after exceeding license limitations

At a business with a direct sales force, product managers can help sales by creating sales collaterals such as product datasheets, white papers, and slide decks. They can also help by accompanying salespeople on sales calls - remotely or in person. Representing your product in front of your customers and demonstrating your expertise can be very effective. You will, of course, want to present a "salesy" version of your product's features and benefits. This entails withholding information about other customers, competitive threats, and implementation woes. While your job is to always tell the truth, you don't have to divulge every detail while participating in sales calls, or you'll quickly lose the privilege.

Another way to help generate revenue is to work with business development on developing partnerships with other players in your ecosystem. This may include technology providers, distributors, system integrators, and companies making complementary products. Many mature B2B companies get most of their revenue through partner sales. Helping sales and biz-dev identify and close partner deals is a great way to advance your product, your company, and your career.

Customer Success

"Get closer than ever to your customer. So close, in fact, that you tell them what they need well before they realize it themselves"

- Steve Jobs

One of the most reliable success metrics for a SaaS business is its customer retention rate: the percentage of customers the company has this year compared to the previous year. This KPI is particularly important given the high customer acquisition costs, especially in competitive markets. Once you acquire and onboard a customer, you don't want to lose them. Salespeople who bring new customers are often called hunters, and those who keep existing ones happy are called farmers. "Farming" customers has evolved into a separate practice called Customer Success. Customer success people help ensure that customers don't churn and ideally spend even more money year after year.

As a product manager, your primary contribution to customer success is in tending to your product homestead and maintaining it at peak performance. As time goes by, you will crank out more and more releases of your existing products to keep them competitive and ensure that they don't die on the vine. The maintenance needs of existing products grow with the continued investment in new features.

It is often much less exciting to maintain an existing - often old - product than to create it in the first place, and this task tends to be less glamorous. Its contribution to customer success is immeasurable, though; if you let your product fall behind, customer satisfaction will fall soon after.

Here's how you can help with customer retention beyond maintaining your product in top shape:

- Participating in review meetings like quarterly business reviews where you will likely be asked to present the product vision and short-term plans.
- Initiating ad-hoc roadmap review meetings for key customers. This becomes necessary when, for example, an account renewal is at risk, and the customer success team is looking to appease a frustrated customer.
- Taking part in customer conferences, also known as customer councils, customer advisory boards, or similar. Bringing customers together for an open discussion about their needs is an excellent retention tool and a strong investment in your company's future.

In one of my previous roles, we would let customers vote on new features. Here's how it worked: at our annual customer conference, we would invite everyone to a large meeting room with flip boards lining the walls, some prepopulated with upcoming features. For about 30 minutes, customers would consider the listed roadmap features and add new ones on the flip boards. During lunch, the product management team would review the list, deduplicate the requests, and put them on clean sheets of paper. We would then give customers five color stickers each and ask them to put a sticker next to each feature they'd like us to add to the product. The key was for us to leave the room and have only customers stay in, letting them discuss and negotiate with each other. After an hour or so, we would come back and review the results. Seeing which feature requests bubbled up to the top was always eye-opening. In many cases, the top ones were not even close to the ones we assumed would end up there.

All these customer interactions will result in a slew of new roadmap features and invaluable information about use cases that will influence strategic plans. Listening to customers and showing a genuine interest in understanding their needs and wants puts you on a solid path toward creating a better product. Getting closer to customers is your most significant contribution to customer success.

Part 5

Collaborating

Working with Others

"We rise by lifting others."
                - Robert Ingersoll

It is often said that the key to business success, particularly for startups and small companies, is Team, TAM, and Time. You can control time - to a degree - by making effective roadmap decisions and optimizing processes. Your TAM (Total Addressable Market) is largely beyond your control, but you can increase or decrease your target market size by changing your focus. Your extended team is where you have the most leverage. In good times, it's their effort that drives your success. When things go south, you can't pin it on other people or factors; you must take responsibility and deal with the consequences.

Product Managers orchestrate the efforts of engineers, designers, operations people, and others without having formal authority over them. These people are your most valuable assets, and motivating them is where your influence skills come into play.

Influence skills are difficult to quantify or describe in a formula or an algorithm. They enable you to make other people do things they wouldn't otherwise do. You can convince most people with solid data, but you're not always lucky enough to have much of it. Your best bet is to hone your influence skills and become exceptionally good at it.

Product managers are the interface between the market and the people who build the product. Unlike what some stingy (but hopeful) executives wish for, it's not easy to get rid of them and have the market "talk" to the implementers directly. In some markets, most notably online products and services where data is abundant, the need for product management is sometimes less obvious. There too, though, product management is an essential function. Even when performed by people with different titles, it's still product management.

Product managers must be able to work with a variety of people in a multitude of roles. As the table below suggests, they need to adapt to different communication styles, speeds, and constraints:

Market	Product Management	Engineering
Moves fast	Buffer	Velocity is directly proportional to resource availability
Changes frequently	Shock absorber; smooths out change	Has inertia; once started, it's costly to change course
Capricious	Sanity checker bounded by business constraints	Stringent sanity checker bounded by feasibility
Generates competitive and other pressures	Studies, anticipates, and plans	Ideally isolated from outside pressures

The people you will likely interact with the most are those who build and sell your product. There is no other option but to be on good terms with them, preferably their friend. You won't always bring them the good news, but a friendly relationship will make whatever message you convey easier to swallow.

While you must have confidence in your human resources, you can't trust them blindly. The key is to trust but verify. As Ernest Hemingway once said, "never confuse movement with action." Learn about the areas they specialize in until you know enough to be dangerous, and gradually build mutual trust through in-depth discussions. Hands-on product managers are the best in the business.

When engineers deliver a product release, close the loop by trying it out yourself. Don't accept their work blindly unless you've known them for years and have complete trust in their output. Speaking their language will allow you to communicate more effectively and know when the right thing is not to bother them at all.

Culture

"Have the serenity to accept the things you cannot change, the courage to change the things you can, and the wisdom to know the difference."
- A secular version of Reinhold Niebuhr's prayer

A positive culture is conducive to efficient product management. Companies that foster a culture of cooperation and mutual respect make the product manager's life much more manageable. Whether or not you have direct reports, you can exert your influence and help build a positive culture for the benefit of everyone involved. Not only will your life be easier, but your product will end up being better.

A culture of personal commitment and timely delivery is vital. If the norm is to miss deadlines, most people will eventually succumb to it. You must fight this, and your best weapon is your own behavior. Build a positive culture while leading by example. Set clear goals and deadlines, challenge yourself to meet them, and your peers will follow suit. Be persistent; it doesn't take much to lose credibility. One serious lapse, and they may lose faith in your sincerity.

Negative emotions like guilt, jealousy, and pessimism won't help you reach your business goals. They can drain your momentum by hampering honest efforts, damaging motivation, and derailing otherwise smooth processes. However, these are natural emotions that many people express in the workplace. Some make a sincere effort to hide them; others are more upfront. If you feel these or similar emotions, find a way to process them. It's ok to be vulnerable with some people, but it may backfire with others.

To get others on board, be an optimist. Don't jeopardize your product by exposing your fears or being jaded. If reality is too grim, change what you have control over. If the problems are too immense, you are doing something wrong. Wrong technology, wrong market, wrong process, wrong team. Whatever it is, something has to give. If you exhausted your ability to affect change after escalating as appropriate, it might be time to look for greener pastures.

Your Team

As a leader, you should spend significant time building and nurturing a strong team that will act as a force multiplier. For a product manager, managing people is a mixed blessing. Having a team means that others share the burden of managing the product, but it's your responsibility to guarantee that everybody is busy and productive. It's up to you to ensure that the fruits of their labor are turned into a consistent product.

Delegating all your work and being hands-off is a terrible idea. It may work for a short while but will backfire sooner or later. If you don't have an unmitigated relationship with the market and hands-on experience with the forming product, you will inevitably lose touch with reality and build the wrong one.

Do

- Listen and facilitate other people's work.

- Develop your team members' careers.

- Ensure that they have the tools they need.

- Be consistent and persistent.

- Streamline communication between your team members and other stakeholders.

Don't

- Micromanage.

- Be neurotic.

- Change your mind too often.

- Be arrogant (leave hubris to the insecure).

- Be jaded.

As a leader, you should make sure that your team members have the freedom and resources they need to do their job. You don't have to be their administrative assistant; not everything should go through you. Instead, help them communicate freely among themselves and with others. Remove yourself from the critical path so that communication can flow more smoothly.

Your team's structure is significant in getting them fully engaged and humming on all cylinders. It's essential to build a balanced team while avoiding Conway's Law: for example, if you assign a product manager to work on a particular initiative, you're almost certainly going to end up with the associated feature set being built, whether or not it's the right thing to do.

Of all your team members, pay special attention to the outliers on both sides of the bell curve. Low performers should be encouraged to improve, moved to a different role, or dismissed if all else fails. This can be challenging, but the other side of the curve is where changes are more difficult to make.

High performers are extremely valuable. Since virtually all employment arrangements nowadays are "at will," you must be on top of your high performers' morale. Retention can become a significant issue if you don't manage it carefully. People typically leave for a combination of three reasons (among others):

1. They are bored.

2. They are fed up with company politics and red tape.

3. They can't get along with their manager.

The first two are fairly easy to spot and, although challenging, relatively easy to fix. The last one is hard to identify and even harder to fix, especially if you don't have a good feedback source. That one is all about you, which makes it an exercise in self-introspection and an excellent reason to have a mentor who can help you see beyond. If you're lucky enough, your manager is also a good mentor. In most cases, you will have to enlist your own confidant, preferably from outside the company, who will serve as your sounding board and shed light on what is otherwise difficult to see by yourself.

Managing Chaos

"'There must be some way out of here' said the joker to the thief 'There's too much confusion', I can't get no relief."
- Bob Dylan,
All Along the Watchtower

Management is the art of creating order in chaotic situations or those bound to end up in chaos. Managers do this in various ways, most of which fall between micromanagement and letting things manage themselves. No matter where you are between these two extremes, you must work against the tongue-in-cheek second law of office thermodynamics, stating that chaos at work can only increase. This is true whether managing processes or people - especially free-spirited knowledge workers.

Micromanagement with frequent course corrections requires setting clear rules and periodically nudging employees and middle managers toward what top management considers the right direction. This drives employees increasingly resentful and disgruntled. On the other end of the spectrum is self-organized chaos - an organization or a system that strives to manage itself. Many startups operate this way. It may look like a mess from the outside, but the added benefit of boundless creativity is significant, and the results speak for themselves.

Self-organized chaos is the best way to get groups of creative people to work toward a common goal. Your challenge as a manager is to let attractors form naturally rather than to create them artificially. You need to articulate long-term business goals and make sure everyone understands them. Beyond that, it's up to your team members to develop innovative strategies and implementation plans. Emergence, the science of how intricate patterns or behaviors emerge from myriad simple interactions without central direction, applies to any sufficiently large group. It can be harnessed by carefully defining and studying the rules that govern the interactions, or in this case: company culture.

The second law of office thermodynamics only applies to closed systems. The more closed a company is, the tighter management has to be in order to control its natural tendency to become chaotic. Opening up and allowing transparency and cross-pollination can lead to more effective self-management and greater stability. It facilitates hands-off management and lets teams self-organize and deliver remarkable results. The key to success is hiring intelligent, creative, and cooperative people who can make things happen. Building openness and freedom into your team's (and company's) DNA is the best way to achieve greatness.

Your Manager and Theirs

"When you're screwing up and nobody says anything to you anymore, that means they've given up on you."

- Randy Pausch

You can rarely choose your boss, but you can learn to live with them and learn from them. If you're lucky, your manager will be a natural role model who takes you under their wing and sees that you get the training and nurturing you deserve. Regardless, you can do your best to absorb whatever they have to offer.

Bosses can be annoying at times, but even if it seems like the only reasons they got promoted are their keen political senses and suck-up skills, there are still some things you can learn from them. You probably want to see yourself in their position one day. What do you need to do to get there? Try to adopt the elements of their success you can live with while avoiding the ones you don't appreciate.

Your manager knows how to do their job but could use your help. Understand their needs and constraints and do your best to assist; this is the essence of "managing your manager." Help them do their job and please their boss; you will learn a valuable lesson about working with your skip-level manager. This is one of the best things you can do if you want to find yourself in their shoes.

Never make your boss look bad, even if you feel that you are competing with them directly. Help them succeed, and their success will rub off on you. If you tried a few times and realized this doesn't apply to your situation, it may be time to move on. Sticking around and serving a self-absorbed, self-serving manager can be a miserable experience.

Company Politics

"One of the penalties for refusing to participate in politics is that you end up being governed by your inferiors."

- Plato

It is only natural for a complex, largely covert lattice of relationships to evolve in any group of people. Businesses act like Petri dishes that grow elaborate networks of interests fueled by the desire for prestige and higher compensation. People foster various kinds of relationships with their peers. Some are friendly, some are aloof, some are jaded, and others are hostile. Relationships form gradually, taking years to gel.

The lattice typically morphs slowly, evolving as people join, leave, or change roles. Most people are reluctant to change much, slowly working their way up the food chain. Others jostle to improve their position. If the lattice has strong ties, these provocateurs will eventually yield, assimilate, or move on.

Sometimes, the subtle balance is disrupted by an earthquake: layoffs, acquisition, fraud, or technological breakthrough. Those enterprising souls vying for a better position become exceptionally expeditious when this happens. They ruffle their feathers and try to work their way up the ladder even faster. When the earth is shaking, some end up at the top of a hill while others sink into a faultline, never to be seen again.

As a product manager, you need to work closely with stakeholders throughout the organization. Your goal is to remain on good terms with everyone, regardless of their company-political affiliation. And don't say you don't do politics; it's like saying you don't have emotions. Although it can feel like negotiating a minefield, you simply have to remain everybody's friend. Prove your management chops by managing your emotions and giving everyone enough of what they want so you end up getting what you need.

Dealing with Brilliant Disruptors

"The only normal people are the ones you don't know very well."

- Joe Ancis

Unless you're at the very edge of the bell curve, you must have had a chance to work with people who are more intelligent than you. Chances are, some of them were a tad difficult to work with. It's easier to deal with a fool who overreacts and blows things out of proportion than with a brilliant person who behaves this way. The latter's actions are likely premeditated, aimed at achieving a particular outcome. Don't believe the theory that some people are just nasty and the corollary that super-smart people can be nastier than others. Every person has a story, and if you sincerely try to understand it, you'll be one step closer to figuring out the reasons behind it - if not outright helping them improve.

Your misbehaving genius may be trying to send you a message, so you better read between the lines. Like many communication issues, it might be a management problem, not a personal one. If you are the manager, your job is to facilitate smooth and friendly communication between all stakeholders. Blaming your problem on other people's psyches won't solve it. Worse, it will reflect poorly on your ability as a manager.

How do you deal with a troublemaker who can outsmart you? First, let's talk about the consequences of ignoring the problem and hoping it will resolve itself. Anyone who has hired smart and capable people knows how hard it is to find them in the first place, meet their expectations regarding employment terms, and retain them for the long haul. When you finally seal the deal, the last thing you want is to lose them. This, however, is exactly what might happen if you blame them for their bad behavior. Don't take their actions at face value; dig deeper and find the cause.

Chances are they are trying to induce some change, and a sensible one to boot. They probably tried a kinder way first - long ago, perhaps - but their attempts fell on deaf ears. Chances are that said change is difficult to make. It might be some confusing and inefficient process they're trying to simplify, some roadblock that other people choose to ignore, or organizational behavior that needs to be modified. Either way, once you figure out what they are trying to say, you can deal with it head-on. If you can do it without talking to the offender, it's probably for the best. Here's why: if you talk to them, they'll likely tell you how to solve the problem and be very particular about the implementation details, some of which may be nearly impossible to carry out. However, if you deal with the core issue yourself and reach a "good enough" solution, they may accept it as a reasonable compromise.

Next time you deal with a similar issue with your resident genius, give this idea a try. Even if it doesn't help, it's guaranteed not to hurt anyone. After all, that change you've made should have probably been made anyway. Once you've implemented it, things should get better all around.

Part 6

Hiring Product Managers

The Product Interview

"You can't judge a fish by looking in the pond.
You can't judge right by looking at the wrong.
You can't judge one by looking at the other.
You can't judge a book by looking at the cover."

— Willie Dixon

Two qualities matter most when hiring product managers: **smart persistence** and **attention to detail**. Experience, education, and technical aptitude are secondary. Finding out if a candidate is persistent (but not annoyingly stubborn) and fanatically detail-oriented is not trivial in an interview setting. After trying different approaches, I zeroed in on a series of questions that consistently helps uncover the truth. I call it the Product Interview. Of all the product management interview questions and styles, this one works best in my experience.

I start by asking the candidate to pick a market area they know and love - anything goes. Some pick space travel, and others choose "trivial" fields like pencil manufacturing. It doesn't matter to me. Next, I ask them to propose a new product that this market needs. The first mistake some candidates make is to come up with a complex product that relies on some emerging technology or otherwise shaky foundations. This choice makes it easier for me to ask the following questions. Unbeknownst to them, however, they are going to sweat much more and regret not going for a simple product.

Now comes the fun part: I zero in on one aspect of the product and keep asking narrower and narrower, deeper and deeper questions about it - to the point of failure. The questions can be about the business model, technological feasibility, time to market, cost structure, social aspects, or anything else. I only stop pushing when one of three things happens:

1. We run out of time.

2. They give up and admit defeat.

3. They start crying (yes, it happened a few times).

This series of successive questions, which can take an hour or so to go through, tells me much of what I need to know about the candidate's most important qualities. On the way, I pick up clues about their other capabilities. Though these interviews can get stressful (for both sides), they help weed out weak candidates who'll end up being bad hires.

About to be interviewed? Try this thought experiment. You can do it anytime, including while driving or walking; no need to be in front of a computer or a whiteboard. In fact, you don't even need to have an upcoming interview. It's an interesting way to think about how the world works and about human enterprise in general.

Imagine a business, any business, and think about how you would turn a profit in that market. Don't limit yourself to the usual suspects like gaming apps or payment processing services. Think out of the box.

Here is an example: a company that builds scaffolding before a contractor installs new siding or a painter puts a fresh coat of paint on the walls. It's an established, labor-intensive market that's been around for ages. Say you inherit this scaffolding company from your great uncle; how would you run it? How would you differentiate yourself? How will you make a profit? Think about the vehicles and tools you'll need.

Think about hiring, training, retention, and workers' compensation insurance. Consider the challenge of advertising your business in a crowded and commoditized space. How will you convince customers that it's better to outsource their scaffolding needs than do it themselves? How will you leverage technology to increase efficiency? How will you position your company when applying for a bank loan?

You can literally spend hours imagining your life as a scaffolding company CEO. You don't need to do any research for this thought experiment to be useful. You've been around long enough, seen buildings being erected and improved, and probably dealt with landlords and contractors. You already know enough about this market to be dangerous.

This is a thought experiment, not a business case exercise, so keep it all in your head rather than creating a slide deck or a business plan. It might be easier for you to do it in a conversation with a friend. They don't have to know anything about the business, just ask you probing questions about it.

Rethinking Domain Expertise

"A specialist is a man who knows more and more about less and less."

                 - *William J. Mayo*

A common hiring mistake is to insist on hiring someone with significant domain experience. While such a hire – if you can find them at all - has its merits, the drawbacks often outweigh them. The common belief, to paraphrase an old meme, is that "no one was ever fired for hiring a candidate with domain expertise." Hiring managers think they play it safe by ignoring "industry outsiders" whose career path has not passed through a specific domain. It is easier to vet candidates who lack certain keywords on their resumes. Rejecting them outright feels right. But is taking the easy route the right way to go?

The perceived upside:

- A shorter learning curve: many businesses deal with sophisticated technologies. Someone who "speaks the language" can presumably hit the ground running. In reality, though, it depends on the individual. Some people are fast learners, while others are slower on the uptake. Regardless of how many years they spent in the industry, your specific business is different from the competition, and a new hire will have to adapt.

- Industry contacts: this is a real advantage, mostly for salespeople. But remember that a Rolodex full of contacts may, in fact, consist of very loose connections – people the candidate had met briefly in a tradeshow, for example, and whom they cannot easily leverage.

- Bringing big company know-how to a smaller one: there's value in that, but the skill set required for succeeding in a large company is very different than in a small one, so it's essential to understand what else the candidate brings to the table.

The downside:

- Needlessly limiting the number of qualified candidates: this is particularly significant in small niche markets but holds true in broader segments as well. Why limit your choice from the get-go if you want to find the best?

- Dogmatic thinking ("been there, done that") - Maintaining stagnant opinions rather than introducing out-of-the-box thinking: poaching a person who "knows the market" from a direct competitor may send ripples of excitement down your spine. Alas, they aren't likely to be a game-changer unless they made significant contributions in taking that competitor to the position your company wants to be in. Besides, the market is now very different, presumably partly due to their efforts.

- Hiring a yes-man rather than someone who will ask tough questions and make things happen: if the candidate hitched a free ride on the competitor's success and is now hand-waving vigorously trying to demonstrate their competence, you're in for a major disappointment.

- Compromising on a sub-par candidate: this is the biggest risk - being dazzled by the candidate's experience while turning a blind eye to their drawbacks.

You should be looking for someone who can learn and evolve while applying their experience to grow the business. A myopic approach to hiring is not going to make your company great. If you are a middle manager trying to protect your turf and survive another day before your promotion is due, this may be the right approach for you.

Any other hiring manager should take a step back and think carefully before writing a line like "Domain expertise – a must" in a job description.

Hire Growers

"Change is inevitable. Growth is optional."

- John C. Maxwell

Tech workers rarely take a job just because they need one. It's a buyer's market for the most part, and more so when the economy is booming. Rational job seekers - and I'd like to think they all are - choose positions that will allow them to grow and develop.

Finding the right person for the job is never easy. The hiring manager's job is to hire people who are most likely to grow and help them realize their potential. The ethical justification for a hiring decision does not revolve around saving the candidate from starvation or allowing yourself to take more days off. Instead, it centers on imagining a better future for the candidate and coaching them on their path to achieving it. Hiring someone only to fill an opening is as short-sighted as getting hired just for the paycheck.

Hiring people who want to grow and develop is the best option for both sides. Growers are people who constantly try to improve what they do and how they do it. Even though they think long-term, they don't necessarily have to be young. Some employers use the euphemism "dynamic" to describe what is essentially a young person, hiding a discriminatory message in otherwise mundane job descriptions. Optimists see "dynamic" as a characteristic of growers of any age.

Growers want to assume increasing responsibility and likely see the hiring manager's position as their next career move. Understandably, hiring them can be intimidating. On the other hand, hiring candidates who are set in their ways is a sure sign of mediocrity; job seekers would be wise to stay away from such employers. As they say, A players hire A players, but B players hire C players. Hiring an A player requires foresight and planning, and, most of all, courage - a rare commodity in many companies.

How do you identify growers? Look for these telltale signs:

- They have a clear vision of their career path and can articulate it.

- They make an effort to understand your market and can envision your company's next moves.

- They have the background required to grow even further.

The next time you're trying to "fill a req," be brave and hire a grower who will take your team (and possibly your company) to the next level. They will likely seek - and may eventually get - your position, but if you manage it correctly, this should propel you toward the next step in your own career.

Hire the Future, Not the Past

*"Cause the good ole days
weren't always good
And tomorrow ain't as bad as
it seems"*

> *- Billy Joel,*
> *Keepin the Faith*

A recent study[7] found that recruiters spend 7.4 seconds scanning a resume before making their go/no-go decision. If true, one possible conclusion is that they focus their scant attention on the most recognizable elements on the page: brand names.

Well-known brands grab our attention and make it easy to categorize candidates by association: "He's a Googler." "She's ex-Microsoft." "Brianna spent five years at McKinsey." We recognize brands like faces, requiring zero time and minimal brain capacity. I see this as a hiring manager (who spends much more than 7.4 seconds going through each resume, to be clear). Like it or not, recognizable brand names immediately catch your attention; you've seen the word "Microsoft" a million times owing to their billions of advertising dollars. This candidate

---

[7] http://cdn.theladders.net/static/images/basicSite/pdfs/TheLadders-EyeTracking-StudyC2.pdf

whose resume you're reading spent some time at that company, but what does it mean for your business? Probably not much.

Brand names are the equivalent of photos on dating apps. People use them as a signal for swiping left or right, but much like people's faces, they provide undeniably superficial cues about the candidate's merits.

In a large company, people can hide and do mostly nothing. I'd like to believe that most people don't, but I know that some do. I've met many hiring managers who think that by working at a large, successful company, the candidate must have soaked in the secret sauce that made that company large and successful and will bring that know-how with them. Good luck with that. One cog does not a machine make.

A hiring manager's real challenge is finding exceptional candidates, regardless of the brand names listed on their resumes. This is hard whether you spend 7.4 seconds or 7.4 minutes evaluating them. You're looking for high performers who'll take you to the next level. These gems often hide in plain sight, having followed a less glamorous career path. Give them the time and respect they deserve.

Hire People with a Plan

*"Living is easy with
eyes closed
Misunderstanding
all you see"*

*- The Beatles,
Strawberry Fields Forever*

Business celebrities like to go on the record describing a killer interview question they always use. I have my own question, and I can humbly claim that it's better than any other I've seen. The question is straightforward: "**What would you like to do when you grow up?**" Before you keep reading, imagine yourself in an interview setting and try to answer this question. Forget about your childhood answer. Back then, you were likely asked what you wanted to *be* when you grew up, not what you wanted to *do*. So, what would you like to do when you grow up?

Got the answer?

Here's how I know this seemingly trivial question is very powerful: most candidates have a hard time answering it. I typically hear one of the following wrong answers:

- "I have no plans; I just play it by ear."
- "I'd like to do pretty much the same stuff I'm doing now."
- "I'm already grown-up" (this is the saddest and "wrongest" one).

I like this question because it gauges the candidate's ability to articulate abstract ideas about their future self. It forces them to think long-term and tell what is hopefully an engaging and touching story that ties their past, present, and future into a single narrative. Some candidates struggle to answer this deceivingly simple question. Rarely do I meet a candidate whose career is well thought out and who is on track with implementing their strategic plan. The fact that most people struggle to come up with a clear strategy is, more than anything, a testament to their inability to understand the dynamics of the business world, tainted by hubris and fear. I don't blame them for that, but I wish more people would have figured this out.

Next time you interview a candidate, ask this question and witness the magic. Use it towards the end of the interview, after you've created some rapport with the candidate. And if you are being asked this question, don't dismiss it with an off-hand answer. Your reply transcends the interview and your tenure at that job. In fact, having a well-thought-out answer is essential for enjoying a better career and a happier life.

Part 7

Ownership

Embrace the Fear

Fear is real. It can instinctively paralyze you or prompt you to fight or run away. In some situations, none of these reactions will get you very far.

Being a product manager involves making decisions that are not for the faint of heart. You must constantly evaluate competitive threats, technological challenges, and partnership risks; some events can be very frightening. Freezing or running away are not viable options. Fighting back isn't necessarily a perfect one, either. In many cases, simply hanging in there is the right strategy. You must learn to live with panic-inducing situations that can break (or make) your product. You must resist the fight or flight instinct and learn to tolerate the risk.

Andy Grove, Intel's influential former CEO, titled one of his books "Only the Paranoid Survive." This summarizes a management philosophy that helped him turn the company into a market leader. There's no doubt that healthy paranoia is essential to running a successful business. The question is how to deal with the intense feelings it evokes and avoid being scarred by it.

If you succumb to the fear, you end up making regrettable mistakes that can kill your business and derail your career. Accept fear as an essential ally on your road to success. It will help you stay the course by keeping you alert. Fear is a strong natural urge, and like many behaviors evolved to keep us alive, it can be managed. Learning to keep it under check is essential for building a successful career while maintaining your sanity.

Some people deal with fear-induced stress through yoga, meditation, boxing, running, walking, or daydreaming. Find a method that works for you and practice it regularly. If it stops working for you, keep looking for better ones. Learning to embrace fear without letting it get to you is essential for maintaining a successful product management career.

Honesty

"I always tell the truth. Even when I lie."

    - Tony Montana, Scarface.

It's not easy to always be honest, but you should make your best effort nonetheless. People rarely admit to lying, but white lies are prevalent. Sometimes, the default reaction to a stressful situation is to fudge the facts. Being dishonest may be easier, but it can make your life miserable.

Lies are often self-justified for business reasons. For example: as a manager, you may find yourself lying to your team about the company's financial condition during a pep talk; nothing too significant, just a slight embellishment of the truth. Even such a slight departure from the facts can backfire, putting you in an awkward position when the actual condition of the business comes to light. Then again, if you know what you're doing, you can probably get away with it. So, should you do it? I believe you should strive not to, but I realize it's not always possible.

It is easier to lie to your customers. Most companies do. However, with the pervasive information flow facilitated by today's technology, it's harder to hide dirty laundry than a decade ago. What buys you a few more days of peace and quiet today can explode in your face next week. Be careful and think long-term.

Do

- Be true to yourself.

- Be honest with your team.

- Tell the truth to your superiors.

- Be open and forthcoming with your customers.

Don't

- Lie, cheat, steal.

- Stab people in the back.

- Be a demagogue.

- Be overly political.

As a product manager, you should have a strong moral fiber and courage to tell truth to power (and everybody else). Tell it as it is rather than delivering an overly optimistic sales pitch or, on the flip side, offering a jaded point of view. The reason is simple: plenty of people provide biased punditry, tell unfounded stories, or outright lie. What the world needs are more truth-tellers who understand reality and articulate it clearly. If reality is grim, find the right time and tone to deliver the message, take a deep breath, and dive in. If things look good, don't make them look better than they are. Honesty pays off in the long run.

Office Space and Time

"People who enjoy meetings should not be in charge of anything."

- Thomas Sowell

Regularly scheduled meetings can be a huge time sink. Some people schedule or participate in meetings in an effort to feel more important or less insecure. This is sad and wasteful at so many levels that something has to be done about it.

Here's an effective method for reducing the number of recurring meetings and the time spent on them. For this to work, you will have to do it in coordination with the real decision-makers in your team, group, department, organization, or company:

1. Raise hell about time wasted in meetings. Put a dollar value on it to make it look really painful.

2. Call a meeting with the decision-makers (and no one else). It sounds ironic, but bear with me.

3. Draw a matrix - rows for required meetings and columns for attendees needed. Forget about optional ones; they are a distraction.

4. Eliminate meetings that aren't absolutely necessary and participants who are not expected to contribute. Passive listeners can always review meeting notes; no need to waste their time and yours.

5. Fill up the matrix, marking an intersection only if this person is essential for that meeting.

6. Decide on frequencies - not every meeting has to happen on a weekly basis. The meeting is probably redundant if you end up with longer than quarterly recurrence.

7. Have the decision-maker(s) announce the change and make sure the new schedules get implemented immediately.

8. Repeat this process periodically to ensure that newly cropped-up meetings are in check.

Enjoy your newly freed-up time.

Cross the Action Threshold

"An ounce of action is worth a ton of theory."

   - Ralph Waldo Emerson

Now more than ever, corporate employees know that every email they send, every document they write, and in many cases, every word they utter is likely being recorded and can be traced back and used against them down the road. This comes on top of their concerns of being criticized, shamed, yelled at, demoted, or fired, which are exacerbated during downturns. And so, people naturally gravitate toward the safe middle ground and refrain from producing original material to stay below the radar. After all, recycling what has already been said, written, presented, or discussed is a safer bet.

Some people's inherent laziness and their desire to "just make it to Friday" drive them toward a default state of inaction. While this can reduce their anxiety like any good old defense mechanism, it can have a devastating effect on their career.

Don't be this person. Don't be afraid to produce creative work. Being original separates middle managers bound to be downsized from critical contributors bound to be promoted. Cross the action threshold – that imaginary line between working for a paycheck to working for the satisfaction of creating the future, between recycling old ideas and minting new ones, between being doubted for pulling your weight to being relied upon for propelling the team forward.

How do you cross that threshold? Here are a few ideas:

- Be brave. Be original. Have an opinion.

- Synthesize information, look for patterns, and leverage them to create new things.

- Self-introspect and be honest about what you do and don't know, then close the gap by learning what you need to learn.

- Be a workhorse, not a showhorse.

- Become really good at what you do.

One positive side effect of crossing the action threshold is your access to mentors. Mentors are in short supply in corporate America (and corporate Anywhere, for that matter). Instead of waiting for a mentor mounted on a white horse to show up and rescue you, be your own mentor as you cross the action threshold: create new things, self-introspect, work hard, and excel at your work. This will turn you into a more attractive mentee, preparing you for when the right mentor comes along.

While concerns of being tracked or shamed can be terrifying and paralyzing, producing original work is an effective brain hack for dealing with these emotions. Try to ignore these thoughts long enough to produce something meaningful.

You are Smarter than you Think

"You're braver than you believe, and stronger than you seem, and smarter than you think."

- A. A. Milne
Winnie the Pooh

There's an epidemic among girls, boys, and adults of all ages. People affected by it proudly declare their perceived disabilities and needlessly berate themselves. I often hear statements like "I'm not smart enough for this," "I'm not good at math," or "I'm not a technical person." Shutting out an entire field of knowledge may help you focus on other areas, but why broadcast it? Why be proud of it? Convincing ourselves that we are not qualified is a defense mechanism, but we shouldn't let it limit us.

I'm not going to restate the age-old new-age mantra "believe in yourself," and I'm not talking about actual disabilities. The sad reality is that intelligent people choose to inflict themselves with a handicap they believe to be real, turning it into a self-fulfilling prophecy. Even people who think they are otherwise highly capable shoot themselves in the foot by joining the cult of self-deprecation.

In fact, I'm still fighting this myself from time to time, especially in situations where I feel the impostor syndrome in full force. It's easy to give up and blame it on some innate inability, but I learned that I'm better than the circumstances often make me think I am. Instead, I strive to identify the crux of the matter and target it with a precision attack, usually by learning a new skill or studying a topic I'm unfamiliar with.

Our always-on, in-your-face culture rewards comparative behavior, and people readily fall into this trap. Some people are better than you at [name any topic], and you will never be the best at it. Social media turns this fact of life into an assault on our senses, making it very difficult to ignore. Too often, people let this spiral out of control, give up on trying to compete, and label themselves a failure.

Being less competitive and less of a perfectionist can do wonders and mitigate the emotional angst involved. The perfect is the enemy of the good, and good is perfectly fine in most cases. Instead of giving up, we should give up trying to be perfect.

Work + Life

"Your work is going to fill a large part of your life, and the only way to be truly satisfied is to do what you believe is great work. And the only way to do great work is to love what you do. If you haven't found it yet, keep looking. Don't settle. As with all matters of the heart, you will know when you find it. And, like any great relationship, it just gets better and better as the years roll on. So keep looking until you find it. Don't settle."

- Steve Jobs

Work-life balance challenges are a side effect of any job. Product managers can get lost in an ocean of details and sink endless hours into work at the expense of their health and social life. Workaholism can be painful, but it's curable.

Working long hours, pulling occasional all-nighters, and spending weekends at the office may be necessary parts of your job. For example, while traveling to all-important customer meetings, you are likely to be away from home for much longer than usual (though the perks of business travel often compensate for that). While you can't avoid putting an extra effort altogether, it's important to vary the time you put into work and your other pursuits. This will make it more manageable and sustainable in the long run and won't tax your health that much.

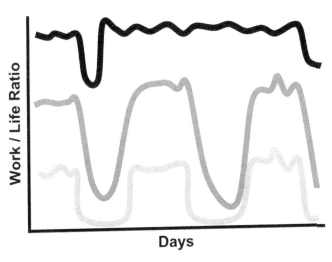

Work-Life balance: the extremes are not sustainable

People tout working long hours for two reasons:

1. Achieving more: This can work in the short term before accumulating a sleep or emotional debt that you'll have to pay back. If you don't change your habits, you may end up with deteriorating health and non-existent social life. Needless to say, substance abuse (excessive amounts of caffeine, energy drinks, or other drugs) is not sustainable.

2. Motivating others: Building enthusiasm and creating excitement are important goals, but working yourself to death is not the best way to produce these results. There are plenty of ways to motivate your team. If you are trying to get low performers to achieve more, talk to them and resolve their specific problems. Beating a dead horse is pointless, and killing yourself in the process is ridiculous.

The best antidote for mindless overwork is to love what you do. You will be significantly more focused and engaged if you're lucky enough to have a job you love. If you're not that lucky, find a different position. Build yourself a career you enjoy rather than a path of suffering. Be true to yourself and identify what you like to do. It's like finding the right product to build - only that you are the product, and your career carries you from one "release" to the next. In your career moves, follow your passion, not only the money (though admittedly, a combination is nice). The next chapter gives a perspective on career moves done right.

Moving In, Moving On

"Life is short and then you die."
- The sad truth

Job hops are inevitable. Employee mobility is one of the reasons innovation centers like Silicon Valley and New York City are so prolific. Moving on after two to three years on the job is pretty common, and no one will be shocked if you do. When you're off to a greener pasture, do it right and don't burn bridges.

Your First 100 Days...

At your old company, you had it cut out for you. Processes were running on autopilot. People trusted you. You knew what everyone was capable of. There were almost no surprises. Oh, the good old days. Now, a short while later, you find yourself in unfamiliar territory - the first day at your new job. You know full well that you will have to prove yourself, and as a product manager, the challenge is significant. The learning curve is steep, no matter what you've done before and how many years of industry-specific experience you have.

The key is to start **producing** as quickly as possible. Show your multi-disciplinary prowess and impress your new coworkers from the get-go. Listen and learn, but don't make this your sole occupation in the first few weeks. Don't just sit there; do something. Making small contributions right from the start will serve two purposes. First, it will show others that you are a proactive leader and help them form a positive opinion about you. Second, it will allow you to test the water and learn how things work in your new company while errors are still forgivable, enabling you to make significant contributions soon after.

...and your Last

Eventually, there will come a time when you decide to leave your company (or somebody decides for you). When moving on, your goal should be to leave on good terms. As they say in the Bay Area: "It's a small valley." Nowadays, however, it's a small world. You are easily findable online, and any bad taste you leave behind may haunt you years down the road. If you initiate the move, tell your boss as early as possible so they can make alternate plans. Do your homework before you talk to them, and get your affairs in order after you do. If at all possible, identify and recommend a replacement (you made a succession plan, right?). Leave everything in good shape, and don't let any task you own fall between the cracks. Hopefully, the processes you put in place will keep humming along for a while until somebody else picks up where you left off.

How to Move Ahead

"If we all worked on the assumption that what is accepted as true is really true, there would be little hope of advance."

- Orville Wright

As we approach the end of the book, I'd like to share a few rules to live by. These helped me move ahead throughout my career, and I hope you'll find them helpful as well.

Focus on what matters

Distance yourself from anything that is not part of the core value creation process. Make meaningful things happen. Don't waste your (or your company's) time and resources.

Have an opinion

No one hired you to shut up. Don't just echo what others are saying. Develop original opinions, and don't keep them to yourself.

Know when to keep quiet

When talking to people who can influence your career, don't say everything that comes to mind. Instead of tooting your own horn, plant seeds by taking meaningful and memorable actions. When the time comes for a promotion or other career moves, you want decision-makers to check with people who remember your impact and arrive at their conclusion based on that.

Be a skeptic

Don't believe your hype, nor others'. Assume that everything you hear is an exaggeration meant to make someone or something look better than they really are. Only after cross-referencing multiple independent sources can you be sure that the information is authentic. Even after you verify it, remember that facts can go stale quickly. Don't base your decision on information that was once true; make sure it still is.

Have a healthy dose of paranoia

Most people are nice and friendly, but a few are out to get you. Disarm them and take the sting out of their schemes rather than fighting them. If you fight, you expose your vulnerabilities and are much more likely to lose (this fight or the next). Win the war before it starts.

Be your own mentor

Having a mentor is great, but don't wait for one to show up. You can find plenty of online and offline resources, like joining meetup groups and consulting with friends and colleagues. However, no one understands you entirely and works solely on your behalf. Be your own mentor and coach yourself to success, leveraging all your resources.

Do your homework

Try harder. Work smart and focus on what's important. Pay attention to details, and don't cut corners. If two people are up for promotion, in most cases, the more productive one will get ahead.

Be prepared

Forget about job security. Love your company? The people? The pay? The location? It can all end in an instant. When you go home in the evening, don't assume you will have a job the next day. This may sound bleak, but it happens all the time. Always have a plan B. Don't burn your bridges, and always keep your eyes open.

Be resilient

Don't give up, but know when giving up is the right thing to do. Don't be afraid to quit. Non-exempt goes both ways. "Have a thick skin," another cliché, is more relevant. Keep calm, and don't let the shit through, no matter how "interesting" things become.

In Closing

Final Musings

When flying above the weather, I can only admire the technology that keeps me aloft. It affords a unique vantage point enjoyed by only a fraction of the billions of humans who ever roamed the earth. The pristine setting and wide-angle perspective remind me of the time before work starts on a new product.

Traveling down from 30,000 feet through clouds of uncertainty until the outlines start revealing themselves, continuing to an altitude of a minimum viable product that evolves into its optimal manifestation. Traveling from "the customer wants x" to "the customer needs y" to "y requires a, b, and c" to "make a, buy b, outsource c" to "thank you for delivering y on time." Traveling with creative experts and artisans from varied backgrounds and cultures, forming a melting pot of talents. From mountains of data through countless iterations of careful analysis to informed decisions. From backstabbing to back rubbing, from isolation to cooperation, from suspicion to harmony, from squeaky gears to a well-oiled machine.

I was fortunate to make this trip multiple times – sometimes as a passenger and often in the pilot's seat. I love repeating these trips from a clean slate all the way to a satisfied customer. The journey never gets old and always offers new challenges. I hope to be fortunate enough to experience it many more times.

Afterword

Now that you've read this book, I hope you'd agree that product management is as important and complex as many other sought-after professions. It's not something "engineers who can talk" do when they get older. A product manager is not a glorified marketer with a technical background, either. They are a professional in their own right, an artisan, and skilled artisans are worth their weight in gold. A good product manager can be the difference between wasting resources chasing a mirage and making a sound investment in winning products. They are catalysts of good processes, capable of turning chaotic situations into impeccable execution engines.

This may sound apologetic, but we product managers don't need to beg for respect. People who dismiss product management do so at their peril. A product manager is a Jack of all trades and a would-be master of all. They could perform any role were they not that busy, but this shouldn't preclude them from learning new skills daily.

To drive progress, researchers need to become increasingly specialized, and engineers must focus on particular technologies. Product managers don't have this luxury. They must be equally comfortable with everything they deal with – sales, marketing, engineering, financial modeling, and quality assurance, among others. Higher complexity makes their lives difficult but not impossible. They don't need to excel at everything; they just need to speak the language and know enough to be dangerous (and then some).

A product manager should ideally be a generalist. Yes, some specialization is required, but in what area? Statistical analysis, so you can draw better conclusions? System architecture, so your product specifications make more technical sense? Computer programming, so engineers don't rebel against you? Graphic design, so you can accurately mock up the product? The short answer is all of the above and much more. You also need to be a pro at project management and people management (even if you don't have direct reports). Having poor knowledge of what is really going on and relying blindly on others is a recipe for disaster. You must work well with others and be self-sufficient at the same time.

Product managers are creators; creators of vision, strategy, design, products, services, and, ultimately, value. A well-rounded product manager has a good understanding of new features, existing features, and obsolete ones. They see the forest and the trees, the past, the present, and the future.

Unlike others, product managers cannot hole up in their cubicles typing away, devoid of context and isolated from outside pressures. Bringing the outside in is, in fact, one of their most important roles. They are like bees flying from flower to flower, collecting nectar; back in the hive, they turn it into honey, all the while working well with others and being nice to the queen bee. Like bees, they return a favor by cross-pollinating the flowers.

Be a creative, proactive busy bee, and you will do well in product management.

Resources

Many topics touched on briefly in this book deserve more in-depth inquiry: positioning, pricing, and data analysis, to name a few. This section lists a few resources, but I encourage you to find others and seek mentors who will help you excel.

Management

- **Crossing the Chasm**: Marketing and Selling Disruptive Products to Mainstream Customers
  by Geoffrey Moore

- **The Goal**: A Process of Ongoing Improvement
  by Eliyahu M. Goldratt and Jeff Cox

- **The Innovator's Dilemma**
  by Clay Christensen

- **The Four Steps to the Epiphany**: Successful Strategies for Products that Win
  by Steve Blank

- **The Lean Startup**: How Today's Entrepreneurs Use Continuous Innovation to Create Radically Successful Businesses
  by Eric Ries

- **Good to Great**: Why Some Companies Make the Leap… and Others Don't
  by Jim Collins

- **Rework**
  by Jason Fried and David Heinemeier Hansson

- **Play Bigger:** How Pirates, Dreamers, and Innovators Create and Dominate Markets
  by Alan Ramadan, Sean Pratt, et al.

- **The Personal MBA**: Master the Art of Business
  by Josh Kaufman

Personal Development

- **Zen and the Art of Motorcycle Maintenance**: An Inquiry into Values
  by Robert M. Pirsig

- **Self-Reliance & Other Essays**
  by Ralph Waldo Emerson

- **The Courage to Be Disliked:** How to Free Yourself, Change Your Life, and Achieve Real Happiness
  by Ichiro Kishimi, Fumitake Koga, et al.

- **The Courage to Be Happy:** Discover the Power of Positive Psychology and Choose Happiness Every

Day
by Ichiro Kishimi, Fumitake Koga, et al.

- **Thinking, Fast and Slow**
  by Daniel Kahneman
- **Predictably Irrational**
  by Dan Ariely
- **Flow**: The Psychology of Optimal Experience
  by Mihaly Csikszentmihalyi

Skill Building

- **To Sell Is Human**: The Surprising Truth About Moving Others
  by Daniel Pink
- **Don't Make Me Think**: A Common Sense Approach to Web Usability
  by Steve Krug
- **Influence**: The Psychology of Persuasion
  by Robert Cialdini
- **Getting to Yes**: Negotiating Agreement Without Giving In
  by Roger Fisher and William L. Ury

Made in the USA
Middletown, DE
07 January 2023

21316217R00129